Reformation Texts
With Translation (1350-1650)

Kenneth Hagen, General Editor

Series: **Biblical Studies**
Franz Posset, Editor

Volume 1

Marquette University Press
Milwaukee, 1994

PRISON MEDITATIONS ON PSALMS 51 AND 31
by Girolamo Savonarola, O.P.

Introduced, Translated, and Edited
by John Patrick Donnelly, S.J.

MARQUETTE UNIVERSITY PRESS
MILWAUKEE, 1994

Cover design by Sean Donnelly,
based on the portrait of Savonarola by
Fra Bartolommeo (1472-1517).

ISBN 0-87462-700-1
Library of Congress Catalog Card Number 94-78952

Printed in the United States of America
© Marquette University Press, 1994

Table of Contents

.

Foreword

Reformation Texts With Translation (1350-1650) (RTT) are published by Marquette University Press, Andrew Tallon, Director. RTT are brief theological and religious works from the fourteenth through the seventeenth centuries translated into English usually for the first time.

The purpose is to provide religious works that are not easily available to those students of this period in need of primary sources and in need of maintaining the languages. We thereby seek to keep alive the tradition of *textus minores.* The criteria for the selection of texts will be solid, intellectual, and exciting material that will entice our students to dig deeper into the primary languages from the Renaissance and Reformation.

The texts are aimed at a wide audience of scholars, students, persons working in religious areas (such as churches or synagogues), as well as at laymen and laywomen interested in pursuing religious readings from the Renaissance. To facilitate their use, each text features the original language and English translation on facing pages.

Latin and German will be our first languages; thereafter, French and Spanish; eventually Greek and Hebrew. Since the goal is not only to make more works (from 1350 to 1650) available in translation but also to encourage scholars to continue in original language study, we will select works done in manageable Latin to begin with.

Three series are currently planned: Biblical Studies, edited by Dr. Franz Posset; Women of the Reformation, edited by Prof. Merry Wiesner-Hanks; and the Late Reformation, edited by Prof.

Robert Kolb. Additional series will be developed as editors and writers are signed on.

Marquette University advisory committee consisted of John Patrick Donnelly, S.J., Professor, History; Edward Maniscalco, graduate student; and Rebecca Moore, graduate student.

Kenneth Hagen
General Editor

PREFACE

In a famous remark Machiavelli dismissed Girolamo Savonarola as a prophet unarmed and hence doomed to failure. He was certainly a political failure, and paid with his life for that failure, but there are many ways to measure success and failure. It was Machiavelli's own failure in politics that led to his career as a writer and to undying fame. It was Savonarola's failure in politics that led to his arrest and imprisonment, but he was not a prophet totally unarmed, for in prison he retained the pen, which is often mightier than the sword. There he wrote the two works printed in this volume. They became the most read of all his writings and prove that physical torture did not destroy his literary and spiritual powers.

Savonarola's exposition or meditation on Psalm 51 (the *Miserere*, Ps 50 in the Vulgate) and Psalm 31 ("*In te, Domine, speravi*," Ps 30 in the Vulgate) have not been printed in English during the twentieth century. The primary purpose of this book is to make that text available in modern English. The secondary purpose is to help students who are trying to learn to read postclassical Latin. As an undergraduate the translator found the Loeb series, which printed the text and translation of classical Roman authors on facing pages, the best single help to acquire facility in reading Latin. Fewer such volumes exist to help students of postclassical Latin. This series tries to fill that gap for both Latin and early modern vernaculars. Savonarola's Latin seems well suited to that purpose because it is fluent and powerful but without great grammatical complexity.

The translator has incurred many debts in his work. He would especially like to thank Professors Kenneth Hagen and Roland

Teske, S.J., of Marquette University, Professor James Kiecker of Wisconsin Lutheran College, and Professor Donald Weinstein of the University of Arizona for help with this project. Dr. Franz Posset caught several slips in the translation and in the transcription of the Latin text and made suggestions which improved the Introduction. Aldemar Hagen did the scanning of the Latin text. The faults remain those of the translator.

John Patrick Donnelly, S.J.
Milwaukee
January 6, 1993

INTRODUCTION

I. Savonarola's Life until His Downfall in 1498

Girolamo Savonarola was born in Ferrara on September 21, 1452, the third of seven children; his early education was guided by his grandfather, a famous physician, who pointed him toward the medical profession. His early studies at the University of Ferrara centered on Aristotle and Thomas Aquinas, but he also became an eager student of the Bible. As a student he brooded on the sins of both laity and clergy; among his writings from these days was a poem "On the Ruin of the World" and a treatise "On the Contempt of the World." Gradually he became so alienated from what he deemed the neopaganism of Renaissance culture and morals that he abandoned his studies, and without even notifying his parents he entered the Dominican novitiate at Bologna in 1475. Of all the religious orders of the time, the Order of Preachers, or Dominicans, gave their candidates for ordination the most rigorous intellectual training, focused on the writings of the great Dominican theologian, Saint Thomas Aquinas. Savonarola returned to his hometown in 1479, where he taught Scripture and the theology of Aquinas for four years.

In 1482 his superiors assigned him to the convent of San Marco in Florence, where he continued to teach and preach. He was esteemed as a devout friar and learned teacher, but his initial sermons achieved only modest success. His Lenten sermons in nearby San Gimignano in 1486 took on a prophetic tone and demanded the reform of the Church lest it suffer God's wrath. In 1487 he resumed his lectures on theology at Bologna, then preached in several minor towns, slowly building such a reputation that in 1490 Lorenzo the Magnificent dei Medici sought

and secured his services for Florence. There he was soon elected prior and preached at San Marco; gradually his sermons attracted such enormous crowds that they had to be moved to the Cathedral. In 1492 Lorenzo died, and his inept son Piero tried to take his place as leader of the oligarchic faction that ruled the city. Beginning in late 1494 Savonarola became a staunch upholder of the Florentine republican tradition against the velvet-glove despotism of the House of Medici.

In 1494 Charles VIII of France invaded Italy to reassert an old French claim on Naples. Piero surrendered to Charles several towns and forts, and Pisa recovered its independence from Florentine domination. Resentment welled up against Piero, and he fled the city. Savonarola welcomed the French King as "the sword above the earth, swift and soon" which he claimed he had predicted would come to purge Florence and Italy of corruption. Later most of the Italian rulers, including Pope Alexander VI, combined against the French invader and forced his ignominious withdrawal from Naples and from Italy. These events left Savonarola the dominant personality in Florence, where he encouraged a more broadly based regime at the same time that he denounced the vices of every level of society. He organized squads of boys to patrol the streets and criticize the sins of adults. More than two hundred novices joined the Dominicans. Starting in 1492 Savonarola's preaching took on an increasingly fiery and apocalyptic tone. Later he claimed that events were unfolding just as God had revealed them to him and as he had partially foretold in his sermons. Often his hearers broke into tears when he attacked their vices. Among his followers were the philosopher Giovanni Pico della Mirandola, the poet Poliziano, and the painter Botticelli. Indeed, sixty years later Michelangelo claimed that he could recall the voice of Savonarola ringing out.

Savonarola incurred the growing hostility of Alexander VI, which had three roots. Prophets who claim a private conduit to God can pose a threat to the traditional hierarchy of the Church.

Savonarola worked to keep Florence from joining that anti-French alliance fostered by the Pope. Finally, the preacher increasingly denounced the vices of the Roman court and of the clergy. Alexander VI, the notorious Borgia Pope, initially praised Savonarola's success in fostering a religious revival. Late in 1495 the Pope ordered Savonarola to preach in Lucca, but he remained in Florence. The Pope then forbade him to preach, but the Florentine government ordered him to resume preaching. Savonarola used the Book of Amos to launch scathing sermons against Alexander and the papal court. He followed these with sermons on Ruth and Micah in the summer of 1496. The Pope offered an olive branch—a promise to make Savonarola a cardinal. This only earned the preacher's scorn. He preached on Ezekiel during the winter of 1496-97. Just before Lent he presided over a bonfire of vanities; his followers threw their cards, dice, pornographic pictures and books, and cosmetics onto a pyre that mounted sixty feet high; around it a ring of Dominicans and their young morals police danced and sang while 20,000 scudi worth of vanities went up in smoke.

A frenetic mood of revivalism is easier to stir up than to sustain. Segments of Florentine society began to turn against Savonarola. One group was those alienated by his puritanism. Another was the merchants who had been the allies of the Medici. The Franciscans, long rivals of the Dominicans, were highly suspicious of his claims to special revelations. Indeed, their suspicions were also shared by his fellow Dominicans living across town at the large priory of Sancta Maria Novella. Alexander VI tried to reorganize the Dominicans into a new congregation of Rome and Tuscany that would put Savonarola more under control of religious superiors, but the friars at San Marco protested and the reorganization was not carried out.

On 13 May 1497 the Pope excommunicated the friar, who rejected the papal brief but refrained from preaching from June until the next February. In this he was encouraged by the

Florentine government, where his enemies now had the upper hand and were fearful that the Pope might lay an interdict on the whole city. On Ash Wednesday of 1498 Savonarola again mounted the pulpit to preach on Exodus and argued that the Pope had ceased to be God's instrument and had lost his authority. Savonarola claimed that he and his followers would fight against the Pope as against the Turks and that they would welcome martyrdom. Martyrdom was not long delayed.

II. Prison, Torture, and Execution

Among Savonarola's supporters none was closer to him or more ardent than his fellow Dominican Domenico Buonvicini da Pescia, who repeatedly offered to undergo an ordeal of fire which would vindicate Savonarola's cause by a miracle. One day a Franciscan offered to accept the challenge. The trial by fire was set for April 7, and for days there was talk of little else in the city. In the Piazza della Signoria in front of the Palazzo della Signoria, or city hall, a long rectangle of firewood was lain down with a narrow corridor down the middle. Long processions of Dominicans and Franciscans lined up to encourage their champions, but there were protracted arguments over technicalities followed by rain. Then government officials ordered the Piazza cleared. Many in the crowd returned home, feeling cheated and bitter because Savonarola had not provided them with a miracle. The next evening an angry mob gathered around San Marco and threatened to burn it. Savonarola's followers came armed to defend the convent. Finally Savonarola surrendered himself to the hostile city authorities to avoid bloodshed. Fra Domenico and Fra Silvestro Maruffi, another close friend, were also taken into custody. The authorities packed the commission with the Friar's enemies to hear the charges. Its purpose was not to weigh evidence but to force Savonarola to confess that he was an impostor.

Alexander VI gave the commission permission to use torture, which normally could not be employed against clerics. The

torture used was the strappado; the victim's hands were tied behind his back, then tied to a pulley which lifted him up, then suddenly dropped him; sometimes the fall wrenched arms from their sockets. The torture had the desired effect on Savonarola; he promised to confess. But when he was returned to his cell he repudiated his confession. He was tortured again. His left arm was dislocated. Again he confessed, again he repudiated his confession or raised objections to specific points. Theoretically he should have written the confession in his own hand, but his arms were too mangled, and he could only sign the document. After torture Fra Silvestro too signed whatever was demanded, but even though his left arm was twice dislocated Fra Domenico withstood the strappado and other tortures and admitted nothing. Savonarola had two trials before the city commission; the second ended on April 24. He also had a short ecclesiastical trial May 20 to 22 before Gioacchino Torriano, the Master General of the Dominicans, and Bishop Francesco Remolines (Remolino) representing the Pope. They found him and his companions guilty of heresy and handed them over to the secular arm for execution.

It was in prison, as his arms and hands slowly recovered while he awaited execution, that Savonarola composed his last writings. Only in this context can their power be appreciated. Savonarola was imprisoned in the Alberghettino, a small room where dangerous political prisoners were kept; it was in the tower atop the Palazzo della Signoria and had a tiny window looking out on the piazza below. At first Savonarola's jailer treated him harshly, but Savonarola was able to convert him, and then wrote for him a six-page *Regola del ben vivere* (*A Rule for a Good Life*). On May 8 word spread through Florence that Savonarola had completed an exposition of Psalm 51, "Miserere mei, Deus" ("Have Mercy on Me, God"). It was promptly smuggled out and published. Next he turned his hand to Psalm 31, "In te, Domine, speravi" ("In You, Lord, Have I Hoped") but had completed his exposition of only the first two verses by May 23. After attending Mass

and receiving communion that morning, Friars Girolamo, Domenico, and Silvestro were led out to a large scaffold and pyre in the Piazza della Signoria. There they were hanged and their bodies burnt.

III. Savonarola the Writer

During his forty-seven years Savonarola was a prolific writer. His writings are being systematically republished on a high level of scholarship in the *Edizione nazionale delle opere di Girolamo Savonarola* by Angelo Belardetti publishers of Rome. The series began in 1955 and was projected for twenty volumes. Volume 17 appeared in 1992, but many volumes are printed in several parts, so that in fact twenty-seven volumes have been published to date. By far the most copious of Savonarola's *Opere* are his sermons, which were based on specific biblical books, although the biblical text often served mainly as a point of departure for Savonarola's sermons. The dates of some of these sermons have already been noted. The sermons are reprinted in the *Edizione nazionale* in this order: Exodus, Ezekiel, Job, Ruth, Micah, Haggai, Psalms,[1] Amos, Zechariah, and 1 John. The text of many sermons derive only from the notes taken by scribes who listened to the preached sermon. If Savonarola planned to publish a work in both Latin and Italian, he usually wrote the work in Latin and translated it into Italian. Savonarola's debt to the scholastic tradition and to Aquinas is most apparent in the volume of his philosophical writings (Volume 14 in the *Edizione nazionale*), but most of his writings were aimed at a broader audience. Volume 8 in the *Edizione nazionale* prints the considerable corpus of his poems.[2] Sometimes he produced a shortened and simplified version of his works. Among his most noteworthy treatises are the *Dialogus de veritate prophetica, Triumphus crucis, De simplicitate christianae vitae*, and *Solatium itineris mei*. The apocalyptic side of Savonarola's preaching and spirituality is best studied through his *Compendium of Revelations*, which he wrote in 1495; it is partly a summary of his

private revelations and partly an apologetic. It was an immediate best seller, running through three Latin and five Italian editions within a year.[3] The visionary and apocalyptic side of Savonarola is conspicuously absent from his two prison meditations on Psalms 51 and 31, and that may go far to explain why these two meditations remained popular during the sixteenth century while interest in the *Compendium* waned.

IV. The Prison Meditations on Psalms 51 and 31

The two works printed here are entitled in the first editions *Expositio in psalmum Miserere mei Deus* and *Expositio in psalmum In te, Domine, speravi,* but readers will immediately recognize that these works are less learned expositions and more prayerful meditations by a man facing a personal crisis. It is surely this devout, inward, personal tone that has appealed to readers for five centuries. The most popular book written in the fifteenth century was *The Imitation of Christ* by Thomas à Kempis, which is the classic statement of the *devotio moderna.* That movement flowed out from the Netherlands and the Rhineland to counterbalance the dryness of late scholasticism and the ritual formalism that characterized so much of Latin Christendom during the late Middle Ages. The inwardness of the soul, which speaks to God and lays bare her fears and hopes, pervades Savonarola's meditations. Savonarola achieves an intensity which surpasses the *Imitation* and perhaps equals Augustine's *Confessions.* The two earlier Psalm commentaries that Savonarola would have known best are those of Saints Thomas Aquinas and Augustine. That of Aquinas was the work of a scholar and exegete bent on explaining the meaning of the scriptural text, largely for its own sake. Augustine's *Enarrationes in Psalmos* took up Psalms 51 and 31 in a series of sermons designed to move the Christian community at Hippo to live the Gospel; Augustine in tone and purpose came closer to Savonarola's meditations than did Aquinas, but even Augustine's exposition does not have Savonarola's immediacy and inwardness. He was

preaching to his flock, Savonarola was speaking to God and trying to steel himself for martyrdom. A fourth great student of the
Psalms was Martin Luther, and Luther valued Savonarola's meditations so much that he published them twice, the first time in
1523 at Wittenberg under the title *Meditatio pia et erudita super
psalmos Miserere mei et In te, Domine, speravi* and a second time
(only Ps 51) in conjunction with his own commentary on Psalms
51 and 130 (Strasbourg: Apud Cratonem Mylium, 1538). A com-
parison of Luther's commentary with that of Savonarola makes it
clear that Luther's voice is mainly that of the teacher and exegete,
while Savonarola's voice is that of a soul calling God from the
depths of personal tribulation.

It was entirely natural that Savonarola should turn to Psalm
51 (Ps 50 in the Vulgate enumeration) after his arrest. This was
the most famous of the seven Penitential Psalms and had played
a prominent place in the Lenten liturgy and Divine Office which
Savonarola and his fellow Dominicans had been chanting in the
weeks before his imprisonment. Traditionally Psalm 51 was
thought to have been written by David just after the Prophet
Nathan had accused him of adultery with Bathsheba and the mur-
der of her husband Uriah (2 Sam 11:1-27; 12:1-23).

Savonarola begins with a brief prologue which stresses his
sinfulness, his lack of human help, and his trust in God as his
only refuge. His exposition takes up one by one the nineteen
verses of the Psalm. The whole takes the form of a prayer to God,
and each prayer takes its point of departure from the wording of
the specific verse. Although God does not respond to his prayer,
Savonarola's prayer contains many quotations from Scripture,
which can be seen as a divine response. He makes no explicit
reference in this meditation to his imprisonment and torture.
The prayer is both intensely personal in tone and general in that
the person praying represents not just the historical Girolamo
Savonarola but *homo viator*, each of us in our fallen condition
seeking God's pardon and help. The opening reflections and pe-

titions stress past personal sinfulness, the burden of original sin, and the hopelessness of the human condition without God's help, but gradually the tone of both the Psalm and of Savonarola's prayer brightens with hope based on God's past deeds of love for his people. Savonarola then presents a number of passages from the New Testament which brilliantly illustrate his skill as a preacher and writer in making the biblical story vivid and relevant. He retells the story of the prodigal son (Luke 15:12-32), of the Canaanite woman seeking her daughter's healing (Matt 15:22-28), of Peter's denial and repentance (Luke 22:54-62),[4] of Paul's persecution of Christians and his conversion (Acts 9:1-22), and of Mary Magdalene (Luke 7:36-46). The meditation ends on a note of triumph, as Savonarola prays that God may have pity on him so that "I may merit to pass over from this valley of sorrow to that glory 'which you have prepared for those who love you'" (1 Cor 2:9).

Savonarola's meditation on Psalm 31 (Ps 30 in the Vulgate), "In You, O Lord, Have I Hoped," is one quarter shorter than that on Psalm 51, but it would have been far longer had he lived to finish it. He only covered the first two verses. The tone and theological content are similar, but the format is very different. His reflections are not so tightly tied to the verses. While parts of the second meditation also consist of direct prayer to God, much of it is a narrative by Savonarola in which he makes several references to his own life as a friar and to his imprisonment, although Savonarola continues to function as *homo viator*, or better as *homo peccator*. Most of the meditation consists of dialogue between him and two female personifications. The first is Sadness (*Tristitia*), "the worst of women" who urges him to despair, suicide, and a hedonism heedless of the next life. She is presented like Bellona, the goddess of war, who comes at the head of a mighty army of his enemies. Her arguments are countered repeatedly by Hope (*Spes*), whom Savonarola calls his mother and presents as a shining figure sweeping down from heaven with divine aid and coun-

sel. At one point Hope directly refutes Sadness. Such feminine personifications were common in Renaissance art, and Hope had a literary predecessor in *The Consolation of Philosophy* by Boethius (Anicius Manlius Serverinus Boethius, c. 480-524); there Philosophy came to comfort the author in prison before his execution, but the consolations Hope offers to Savonarola owe nothing to philosophy and are entirely religious and biblical. Earlier the meditation on Psalm 51 had contrasted the empty wisdom of the philosophers with the wisdom God gives to his little ones through grace.

In neither meditation does Savonarola refer to any nonbiblical persons or make any explicit literary references outside the Bible. He does not refer to his supporters or tormentors or to the two friars who shared his fate. He makes no attempt to defend his cause, either to himself or to God, much less to posterity. Rather he confesses his sins and failures and begs for God's forgiveness. He entertains no delusions about being rescued by his supporters or released by his enemies. He puts his trust in God as his sole refuge; his hope is in God's mercy and Christ's resurrection; and he neither expects nor seeks vindication in this world or by this world's standards. In contrast to the absence of other literary sources, references to Scripture are ubiquitous, particularly to the Psalms, which he would have virtually memorized from the daily singing of the Divine Office. Minor slips or departures from the Vulgate suggest that Savonarola did not have a Bible at hand as he was writing and that he was quoting from memory—which makes even more impressive his command of the biblical texts which embellish and authenticate his meditations.

V. The Psalm Meditations after Savonarola's Death

The Florentine authorities who executed Savonarola could not so easily destroy the reverence in which many Florentines continued to hold him.[5] The best evidence of his continued popularity was the publication of new editions of his writings after his

death. Publishers in the sixteenth century, even more than today, were driven by the profit motive, so that works which could not command an audience quickly went out of print. Sometimes censorship interfered with the free market. Paul IV, the most conservative of the Counter-Reformation popes, called Savonarola another Luther and wanted the Index of Prohibited Books to include all his works, but only a dozen sermons and one book, *Dialogus de veritate prophetica*, were officially prohibited.[6]

The two works printed here proved over the centuries to be Savonarola's most popular writings by a wide margin. The places of publication indicate that their popularity was not confined to Italy, for they were reprinted in many lands and translated into several languages.

The manuscript of the *Miserere*, or Psalm 51, was smuggled out of Savonarola's prison and first published in Ferrara, his hometown. By the end of 1500 there were eight Latin editions and five Italian editions in print. Its popularity continued during the sixteenth century, although it fell off sharply after 1580. The seventy editions published during the sixteenth century suggest a wide range of readership. Thirty-one were in the Latin original, six in Italian, six in Flemish, and seven in Spanish.[7] The first English translation was by William Marshall; it was printed nine times between 1534 and 1540, but was never reprinted later. There were eleven editions in German; all those printed after 1517 whose place of publication is known were printed in cities dominated by Lutherans. Luther's own fondness for the work has already been noted. Most of the Latin editions were printed in Catholic countries, but many of these too were from Protestant cities.

The absence of a French translation in the sixteenth century is surprising. The first French translation appeared in 1604 and was by Philippe de Mornay, who was nicknamed "The Huguenot Pope." A Jesuit published the second French translation, and the press of the Roman Sacred Congregation of the Propagation of the Faith published a Latin edition. Clearly the appeal of

Savonarola's *Miserere* cut across confessional lines. The same was true of his meditation on Psalm 31. Why? Savonarola was fundamentally an orthodox Catholic, trained in the Thomist tradition and largely untouched by the new humanism of the Florentine Renaissance. It was his bent for apocalyptic prophecy that was most likely to alarm conservative Catholic churchmen. After the Anabaptist experiments at Münster in 1534 and 1535, most Protestant leaders would have been equally wary of this tendency. But that aspect of Savonarola's thought is absent from the two prison meditations. Protestants could only applaud their deep inward piety and their emphasis on Scripture. Moreover both meditations stress human helplessness in the face of sin and utter dependence on God's saving grace. Both works contain passages that seemed eminently consonant with Luther's teaching on justification. Finally Savonarola's denunciations of simony and lust must have endeared him to Protestants, even though they were directed against the sins of Alexander VI rather than against the papacy as an institution. His execution at the hands of Florentine magistrates and papal agents crowned him with the aura of martyrdom.[8]

During the seventeenth century there were only seven editions of the *Miserere*, five in Latin and two in French. There were none at all in the eighteenth century, the Age of the Enlightenment. The work enjoyed a modest revival in the nineteenth century: one Latin, one French, two German, and two English editions. One of the English editions was printed in Milwaukee, the other (Latin-English) at Cambridge University from a manuscript discovered at Corpus Christi College. In the twentieth century there have been four Italian, four German, four French, and one Latin edition prior to this book.[9]

Savonarola's unfinished meditation on Psalm 31, "In te, Domine, speravi," has proven to be the second most reprinted of his works. There have been eighty editions prior to this one. The first Latin edition was printed at Milan in 1499. The next year

there were five more Latin editions, each from a different city. In 1499-1500 there were four Italian editions. During the course of the sixteenth century forty-eight more editions were published, but none after 1580. Some of these were printed with the *Miserere*. The sixteenth-century editions break down as follows: Latin 24, English 9 (all between 1535 and 1540), German 5, Italian 4, Flemish 4, Spanish 2. In the seventeenth century there were only five, four in Latin and one in French (again, by Mornay). There were no editions in the eighteenth century. In the nineteenth century there were five: German 2, Latin 1, French 1, English 1 (again, the Cambridge manuscript). In the twentieth century the breakdown has been: French 4, Italian 3, Latin 1, German 1, and Polish 1.[10]

VI. About This Edition

The Latin text printed in this edition is reprinted with the publisher's permission from the *Edizione nazionale* of Savonarola's works, Volume 12, Part 2: Mario Ferrara, editor, *Operette spirituali* (Rome: Angelo Belardetti, 1976), pages 196-262. The translator made his own translation of biblical quotations from Savonarola's Vulgate because modern English translations vary considerably from the Vulgate, and Savonarola's development is often tied closely to the Vulgate reading. Direct quotations from the Bible have been identified by chapter and verse (following the enumeration of chapter and verse used in the Revised Standard Version), but biblical phrases are so woven into Savonarola's vocabulary that it seemed distracting to try to put them all in. Most Latin sentences begin with a connective, *ergo, itaque, sed, at, autem,* and a dozen others. Modern English is not written that way, so many of the connectives have been dropped in the translation. Many longer Latin sentences have been divided in the translation, as have longer paragraphs.

Selected Bibliography

This bibliography emphasizes works available in English. Those seeking more detailed guidance to the vast literature about Savonarola should begin with Ferrara's bibliography (1981) and Weinstein's review of the literature (1991) listed below.

Bedoyer, Michael de la. *The Meddlesome Friar and the Wayward Pope.* New York: Hanover House, 1958.

Bergkamp, Urban. "Savonarola in the Light of Modern Research." *Catholic Historical Review* 2 (1925): 369-409.

Calogero, Cassandra. *Gli avversari religiosi di Girolamo Savonarola.* Rome: Editrice Studium, 1935.

Cordero, Franco. *Savonarola,* 4 vols.: I. *Voce calamitosa, 1452-1494*; II. *Profeta delle meraviglie, 1494-1495*; III. *Demiurgo senza politica, 1496-1497*; IV. *Agonista perdente, 1497-1498.* Bari, 1986-1988.

De Maio, Romeo. *Savonarola e la curia romana.* Rome: Edizione di Storia e letteratura, 1969.

Erlanger, Rachel. *The Unarmed Prophet: Savonarola in Florence.* New York: McGraw-Hill, 1988.

Ferrara, Mario. *Nuova bibliografia savonaroliana.* Vaduz: Topos, 1981.

Gieraths, Gundolf, ed. *Savonarola: Ketzer oder Heiliger?* Freiburg: Herder, 1961.

Goukowski, M. "Réponse à M. Robert Klein." *Bibliothèque d'Humanisme et Renaissance* 25 (1963): 222-25.

Klein, Robert. "La dernière méditation de Savonarola." *Bibliothèque d'Humanisme et Renaissance* 23 (1961): 441-48.

Lucas, Herbert. *Fra Girolamo Savonarola.* London: Sands, 1906.

McGinn, Bernard, ed. *Apocalyptic Spirituality.* New York: Paulist Press, 1979.

Nolte, Josef. "Evangelicae doctrinae purum exemplum: Savonarolas Gefängnismeditationen im Hinblick auf Luthers theologische Anfänge." *Kontinuität und Umbruch: Theologie und Frömmigkeit in Flugschriften und Kleinliteratur an der Wende vom 15. zum 16.*

Jahrhundert. Josef Nolte, et al., eds. Stuttgart: Klett-Cotta, 1978: 59-92.

Passen, Pierre van. *The Crown of Fire: The Life and Times of Girolamo Savonarola.* London: Hutchinson, 1960.

Reeves, Marjorie. *The Influence of Prophecy in the Later Middle Ages: A Study in Joachism.* Oxford: Oxford University Press, 1969.

Ridolfi, Roberto. *The Life of Girolamo Savonarola.* Trans. Cecil Grayson. London: Routledge and Kegan Paul, 1959.

_____. *Studi savonaroliani.* Florence: Olschki, 1935.

Savonarola, Girolamo. *Operette spirituali.* Ed. Mario Ferrara. Rome: Angelo Belardetti editore, 1955.

Schevill, Ferdinand. *Medieval and Renaissance Florence.* New York: Harper and Row, 1961.

Steinberg, Roland M. *Fra Girolamo Savonarola, Florentine Art, and Renaissance Historiography.* Athens, Ohio: Ohio University Press, 1977.

Villari, Pasquali. *The Life and Times of Girolamo Savonarola,* 2 vols. Trans. Linda Villari. London: Fisher and Unwin, 1899.

Weinstein, Donald, "*The Art of Dying Well* and Popular Piety in the Preaching and Thought of Girolamo Savonarola." *Life and Death in Fifteenth-Century Florence.* Marcel Tetel, et al., eds. Durham, NC: Duke University Press, 1989: 89-104.

_____. "Explaining God's Acts to His People: Savonarola's Spiritual Legacy to the Sixteenth Century." *Humanity and Divinity in Renaissance and Reformation: Essays Presented to Charles Trinkaus.* John W. O'Malley, et al., eds. Leiden: E.J. Brill, 1993: 205-25.

_____. "Hagiography, demonology, biography: Savonarola Studies Today." *The Journal of Modern History* 63 (1991): 483-503.

_____. *Savonarola and Florence. Prophecy and Patriotism in the Renaissance.* Princeton: Princeton University Press, 1970.

_____. "Savonarola—Preacher and Patriot." *History Today* 39 (November 1989) 30-36.

NOTES

1. Savonarola's *Prediche sopra i salmi* (Rome: Belardetti, 1974) include only the first thirty psalms, so it is not possible to compare the works printed here (on Pss 51 and 31) with Savonarola's sermons on the same psalms. There are two obvious differences between his sermons on the psalms and the Latin works printed and translated in this volume. The sermons were written in Italian and directed at a popular audience. The works printed here are much more personal in character.

2. Savonarola disliked the elaborate polyphony being imported into Florence from the Netherlands in the late fifteenth century. His followers preferred to sing more simple hymns or *laude*, which stressed the meaning of the words, usually in the vernacular. Some of these were written by Savonarola himself. After his execution his followers wrote *laude* honoring him, some of which remained in use for a century after his death. On this subject see Patrick Macey, "The Lauda and the Cult of Savonarola," *Renaissance Quarterly* 45 (1992) 439-83.

3. Bernard McGinn, Apocalyptic Spirituality (New York: Paulist Press, 1979) 188; McGinn prints his translation of the *Compendium of Revelations*, pp. 192-275.

4. In his *The Life of Girolamo Savonarola*, trans. Cecil Grayson, (London: Routledge and Kegan Paul, 1959), p. 261, Roberto Ridolfi suggests that Savonarola's treatment of Peter's denial may have hinted to his followers that his own confessions extracted under torture and his recantation of his prophecies should be discounted. Savonarola asks what Peter would have done under torture and replies, "Certainly Peter would have stopped at nothing so that he could free himself ... by denials and lies."

5. Macey, 439-83; the last chapter of Donald Weinstein's *Savonarola and Florence. Prophecy and Patriotism in Renaissance Florence* (Princeton: Princeton University Press, 1970) explores Savonarola's posthumous popularity, pp. 317-73.

6. Macey, 448-49. Paolo Simoncelli, *Evangelismo italiano del Cinquecento: Questione religiosa e nicodemismo politico* (Rome: Istituto storico italiano per l'età moderna e contemporanea, 1979) also discusses the investigation of Savonarola's works under Paul IV: p. 26. Simoncelli devotes several pages to the influence on Luther of Savonarola's prison meditations (pp. 6-9) but has a whole chapter "Savonarola e Evangelismo" which explores Savonarola's influence on the *spirituali* (pp. 1-42). Most of the *spirituali* developed doctrines of justification with affinities to Luther's teaching, but most of them remained Catholics (e.g., Cardinals Gasparo Contarini, Reginald Pole, Giovanni Morone, Girolamo Seripando) but some fled Italy and became Protestant (e.g., Bernardino Ochino and Peter Martyr Vermigli). The best introduction to the literature on this much disputed phase of Italian religious history is Anne Jacobson Schutte's "Periodization of Sixteenth Century Italian Religious History: The Post-Cantimori Paradigm Shift," *The Journal of Modern History* 61 (1989) 269-84.

7. Several vernacular translations also printed the Latin text; these are counted here only once, among the vernacular versions.

8. In his preface (WA 12: 248) to his 1523 edition Luther speaks of Savonarola as "a holy man ... Christ canonizes him." He compared Savonarola's execution to that of the Lutheran protomartyrs who had recently been killed at Brussels by the government of Charles V: (WA 12: 246). In his *Assertio omnium articulorum* ... against the Bull of Leo X in 1520 Luther stated that it seemed that Savonarola should be counted among the saints that the popes had executed: (WA 7: 139). Luther repeated that same claim the next year (WA 7: 439).

Josef Nolte has examined closely Luther's relationship to Savonarola and the prison meditations: "Evangelicae doctrinae purum exemplum: Savonarolas Gefängnismeditationen im Hinblick auf

Luthers theologische Anfänge," in Josef Nolte et al. editors, *Kontinuität und Umbruch: Theologie und Frömmigkeit in Flugschriften und Kleinliteratur an der Wende vom 15. zum 16. Jahrhundert* (Suttgart: Klett-Cotta, 1978), 72-92. Nolte cautiously suggests that "Savonarola's prison meditations have played a role that has been until now undiscovered in the process of Luther's theological self-discovery" (p. 80). He points to Savonarola's closing reflections on verse 2 of Psalm 51, which downplay merit and stress the gratuity of salvation and of God's justice which works through the grace of Christ without the works of the law (p. 81).

Donald Weinstein in his "Explaining God's Acts to His People: Savonarola's Spiritual Legacy to the Sixteenth Century" in John W. O'Malley, et al., editors, *Humanity and Divinity in Renaissance and Reformation: Essays in Honor of Charles Trinkaus* (Leiden: E. J. Brill, 1993) 205-25, thinks (p. 224) that Nolte's focus is too narrowly on the prison meditations and that Savonarola's overall teaching on grace and justification follows that of Thomas Aquinas. I would add the fact that the prison meditations were repeatedly published in Catholic cities during the Counter-Reformation, where they would not have passed the censorship of the inquisitors if they contained a fully Protestant doctrine of justification by faith alone, especially since they were written by a friar executed for heresy.

9. The data for the discussion of the various editions are drawn from the lists of editions printed by Mario Ferrara in his edition of Savonarola's *Operette spirituali*, Vol. 12, Part 2, of the *Edizione nazionale* (Rome Angelo Belardetti editore, 1976) 343-44, 361-70.

10. Ibid., 400-01, 406-12.

Expositio in Psalmum "Miserere mei, Deus"

Exposition of the Psalm "Have Mercy on Me, O Lord"

Expositio in Psalmum
"Miserere mei, Deus"

Infelix ego, omnium auxilio destitutus, qui caelum terramque
offendi! Quo ibo? Quo me vertam? Ad quem confugiam? Quis
mei mirerebitur? Ad caelum oculos levare non audeo, quia ei
graviter peccavi. In terra refugium non invenio, quia ei scandalum
fui. Quid igitur faciam? Desperabo? Absit. Misericors est Deus;
pius est Salvator meus. Solus igitur Deus refugium meum: ipse
non despiciet opus suum; non repellet imaginem suam. Ad te
igitur, piissime Deus, tristis ac moerens venio, quoniam tu solus
spes mea, tu solus refugium meum. Quid autem dicam tibi, cum
oculos elevare non audeam? Verba doloris effundam; misericordiam tuam implorabo et dicam:

"Miserere mei, Deus, secundum magnam misericordiam
tuam Deus qui lucem habitas inaccessibilem."
Deus absconditus, qui oculis corporeis videri non potes, nec
intellectu creato comprehendi, nec lingua hominum seu
angelorum explicari; Deus meus, te incomprehensibilem quaero,
te ineffabilem invoco, quicquid es, qui ubique es. Scio enim te
esse summam rem: si tamen es res et non potius omnium rerum
causa, si tamen et causa. Non enim invenio nomen quomodo
tuam ineffabilem maiestatem nominare queam. Deus, igitur, qui
es quicquid in te est, tu es enim ipsa sapientia tua, bonitas tua,
potentia tua et summa felicitas tua. Cum, itaque, et tu sis
misericors, quid es nisi ipsa misericordia? Quid autem sum ego
nisi ipsa miseria? Ecce ergo Deus misericordia, ecce miseria coram
te! Quid facies, O misericordia? certe, opus tuum. Numquid
poteris recedere a natura tua? Et quid opus tuum? miseriam tollere,

EXPOSITION OF THE PSALM
"HAVE MERCY ON ME, O LORD"

I am unhappy and stripped of all help, for I have sinned against heaven and earth! Where shall I go? Where shall I turn? To whom shall I flee? Who will take pity on me? I dare not raise my eyes to heaven, for I have sinned seriously against it. I find no refuge on earth, because I have been a scandal to it. What then shall I do? Shall I despair? Far be it. God is merciful, my Saviour is kind. God alone then is my refuge: he will not despise his work, he will not cast away his image. I come to you, most kind God, sad and sorrowing, for you alone are my hope, you alone are my refuge. But what shall I say to you, when I dare not lift up my eyes? I shall pour forth words of suffering; I will beg your mercy and say:

"Have mercy on me, O God, according to your great mercy" [Ps 51:1].

The God who "dwells in inaccessible light" [1 Tim 6:16], a hidden God: You cannot be seen by bodily eyes nor grasped by created intellect, nor explained by the tongue of men or of angels. My God, I seek you the incomprehensible, I call upon you the indescribable, whatever you are, who are everywhere. For I know that you are the supreme reality—if you can be called a reality and not rather the cause of all reality—if you can be called a cause. I find no name by which I can name your indescribable majesty. God, you are then whatever is within you, you are your own wisdom, your own goodness, your own power, and your own supreme happiness. Since then you are also merciful, what are you except mercy itself? But what am I except misery itself? Behold then, O God of mercy, behold the misery before you! What will you do, O Mercy? Your own work certainly. Can you

homines miseros sublevare. Ergo, miserere mei, Deus. Deus, inquam, misericordia, tolle miseriam meam, tolle peccata mea: haec enim sunt summa miseria mea. Subleva me miserum; ostende in me opus tuum; exerce in me virtutem tuam. "Abyssus abyssum invocat": abyssus miseriae invocat abyssum misericordiae; abyssus peccatorum invocat abyssum gratiarum. Maior est abyssus misericordiae quam abyssus miseriae. Absorbeat, igitur, abyssus abyssum: absorbeat abyssus misericordiae abyssum miseriae. Miserere mei, Deus, secundum magnam misericordiam tuam: non secundum misericordiam hominum quae parva est, sed secundum tuam quae magna est, quae immensa est, quae incomprehensibilis est, quae omnia peccata in immensum excedit: secundum istam magnam misericordiam tuam, qua sic "dilexisti mundum ut Filium tuum unigenitum dares." Quae maior misericordia esse potest? quae maior caritas? Quis desperare potest? quis non confidere? Deus factus est homo et pro hominibus crucifixus. Miserere ergo mei, Deus, secundum hanc magnam misericordiam tuam, qua Filium tuum pro nobis tradidisti, qua per ipsum peccata mundi abstulisti, qua per crucem eius omnes homines illuminasti, qua "ea quae in caelis sunt et quae in terris" per ipsum restaurasti. Lava me, Domine, in sanguine eius; illumina me in humilitate eius; instaura me in resurrectione eius. Miserere mei, Deus, non secundum parvam misericordiam tuam: parva enim misericordia tua est cum homines a corporalibus miseriis sublevas, magna autem quando peccata dimittis et homines per gratiam tuam super altitudinem terrae sustollis. Ita, Domine, miserere mei secundum hanc magnam misericordiam tuam, ut me ad te convertas, ut peccata mea deleas, ut per gratiam tuam me iustifices.

back away from your own nature? And what is this work of yours? To take away misery, to lift up humans from their misery. Then have mercy on me, O God. I say, by your mercy, O God, take away my misery, take away my sins: they are indeed my supreme misery. Lift me up from my misery, manifest your work in me, exercise your power in me. "Abyss calls to abyss" [Ps 41:8]. The abyss of misery calls to the abyss of mercy; the abyss of sins calls to the abyss of graces. The abyss of mercy is greater than the abyss of misery. So may abyss swallow abyss: may the abyss of mercy swallow the abyss of misery.

Have mercy on me, O God, according to the greatness of your mercy: not according to the mercy of humans, which is small, but according to your mercy which is great, which is beyond measure, which is beyond comprehension, which surpasses all sins to an immense degree: according to that great mercy of yours, by which you "so loved the world that you gave your only begotten Son" [John 3:16]. What greater mercy could there be? What greater charity? Who then can despair? Who not have confidence? God became man and was crucified for us. Have mercy on me then, O God, according to this great mercy of yours by which you handed over for us your Son, by which you took away the sins of the world through him, by which you enlightened all men through his cross, by which you restored through him "the things which are in heaven and which are on earth" [Eph 1:10]. Wash me, O Lord, in his blood; enlighten me in his humility, restore me in his resurrection. Have mercy on me, O God, not according to your little mercy, for your mercy is little when you lift men from their bodily miseries but great when you forgive sins and you lift up men through your grace above the heights of the earth. So have mercy on me, O God, according to this great mercy of yours, that you turn me toward you, so that you blot out my sins, so that you justify me through your grace.

"Et secundum multitudinem miserationum tuarum dele iniquitatem meam."

Misericordia tua, Domine, est abundantia pietatis tuae, qua miseros pie respicis. Miserationes autem tuae sunt opera et processus misericordiae tuae. Venit Maria Magdalena ad pedes tuos, bone Iesus; lacrimis eos lavit, capillis abstersit; indulsisti ei, et in pace eam remisisti. Haec una miseratio tua, Domine. Petrus negavit et cum iuramento detestatus est te: respexisti eum; amare flevit et indulsisti ei, et principem apostolorum eum confirmasti. Haec iterum miseratio tua, Domine. Latro in cruce unico verbo salvatus est. Paulus in persecutionis fervore vocatus, statim Spiritu Sancto repletus est. Hae sunt miserationes tuae, Domine. Deficeret autem tempus, si omnes miserationes tuas enumerare vellem. Quot enim iusti, tot miserationes. Nullus gloriari potest in semetipso. Veniant omnes iusti sive in caelo sive in terra et interrogemus eos coram te an in virtute sua salvi facti sint: certe omnes uno corde, uno ore, respondebunt: "Non nobis, Domine, non nobis, sed nomini tuo da gloriam super misericordia tua et veritate tua." "Nec enim in gladio suo possederunt terram, et brachium eorum non salvavit eos, sed dextera tua et brachium tuum et illuminatio vultus tui, quoniam complacuisti in eis": idest, non ex meritis eorum, non ex operibus eorum salvati sunt, ne quis gloriari possit, sed quoniam ita placitum est coram te. Quod et expressius de se Propheta dixit, cum ait: "Salvum me fecit, quoniam voluit me." Cum itaque tu sis idem Deus "apud quem non est transmutatio nec vicissitudinis obumbratio," et nos creaturae sicut et patres nostri, qui ex concupiscentia nati sunt peccatores sicut et nos, "unusque sit mediator Dei et hominum Christus Iesus," qui manet in aeternum, cur miserationes tuas non effundis super nos,

"According to the multitude of your mercies blot out my iniquity" [Ps 51:1].

Your mercy, O Lord, is the abundance of your kindness by which you look down with kindness on the wretched. But your acts of compassion are the work and outreach of your mercy. Mary Magdalene came to your feet, O good Jesus; she bathed them with her tears, she dried them with her hair; you forgave her and sent her away in peace. This was one of your acts of compassion, O Lord. Peter denied and denounced you with an oath: you looked upon him; he wept bitterly, and you forgave him and reestablished him as the prince of the Apostles. This was another of your acts of compassion, Lord. The thief on the cross was saved by a single word. Paul was called in his zeal for persecuting and was immediately filled with the Holy Spirit. These, O Lord, are your acts of compassion. If I should want to recount all your acts of compassion, time would fail. Your acts of compassion are as numerous as there are just persons. None can glory in himself. Let all the just, whether in heaven or on earth, come forward, and we shall question them before you whether they were saved by their own power. All will certainly answer with one heart and one voice: "Not to us, O Lord, not to us, but to your name give glory because of your mercy and your truth" [Ps 115:1]. "They did not come to possess the land by their sword, and their arm did not save them, but your right hand and your arm and the light of your countenance, because you took delight in them" [Ps 44:3]: that is, they are not saved by their own merits, not by their own works, lest someone be able to take pride, but because it so pleases you. This is what the prophet told more explicitly when he said: "He saved me because he wanted me" [Ps 18:19].

But then you are the same God "before whom there is no change or shadow of alteration" [Jas 1:17], we are creatures just like our fathers, who were born sinners just like us because of concupiscence, and as "there is one mediator between God and humans, Christ Jesus" [1 Tim 2:5], who remains forever, why do

quemadmodum effudisti super patres nostros? An oblitus es nostri? an nos soli peccatores? an non pro nobis mortuus est Christus? an amplius nullae supersunt misericordiae? Domine Deus meus, te rogo, te obsecro: dele iniquitatem meam secundum multitudinem miserationum tuarum, nam multae et infinitae sunt miserationes tuae. Una sufficit mihi, ut videlicet secundum multitudinem miserationum tuarum deleas iniquitatem meam; ut, sicut innumerabiles peccatores traxisti, suscepisti et iustos reddidisti, ita me trahere, suscipere et iustum per gratiam tuam reddere, digneris. Secundum, igitur, multitudinem miserationum tuarum dele iniquitatem meam. Absterge cor meum ut, omni iniquitate deleta ac omni immunditia expulsa, fiat sicut tabula munda, in qua digitus Dei legem caritatis suae scribat, cum qua habitare nulla potest iniquitas.

"Amplius lava me ab iniquitate mea et a peccato meo munda me."

Fateor, Domine, semel delesti iniquitatem meam; delesti iterum; lavasti me milies. Adhuc lava me ab iniquitate mea, quia iterum cecidi. Numquid ad certum numerum parcis homini peccatori, qui Petro interroganti: "Quotiens peccabit in me frater meus et dimittam ei septies?" respondisti: "Non dico tibi septies sed et septuagies septies," numerum finitum pro infinito accipiens? Numquid, ergo, indulgentia superaberis ab homine? Quin immo Deus, magnus Dominus, et "universa vanitas omnis homo vivens"; et solus Deus bonus: "omnis autem homo mendax." Nonne tu dixisti: "In quacumque die ingemuerit peccator, 'omnium iniquitatum eius non recordabor'"? Ecce ego peccator ingemisco, quia "corruptae sunt cicatrices meae a facie insipientiae meae. Miser factus sum et curvatus sum usque in finem. Tota die contristatus ingredior ad te. Afflictus sum et humiliatus sum valde.

you not pour forth upon us your acts of compassion, just as you poured them forth on our fathers? Have you forgotten us? Are we only sinners? Did not Christ die for us? Are there no mercies left anymore? Lord my God, I ask you, I beg you: blot out my iniquity according to the multitude of your acts of compassion, for your acts of compassion are many and infinite. One is enough for me, namely so that you then blot out my iniquity according to the multitude of your acts of compassion; so that, even as you have attracted countless sinners, you have lifted them up and made them just, so deign to attract me, to lift me up, and to make me just through your grace. Blot out, then, my iniquity according to the multitude of your acts of compassion. Wipe clean my heart so that when all iniquity has been blotted out and all uncleanness driven out, it may be a clean tablet on which the finger of God may write the law of his charity, with which no iniquity can dwell.

"Wash me yet more from my iniquity and cleanse me from my sin" [Ps 51:2].

I confess, O Lord, that you blotted out my sin one time, you blotted it out again, you washed me a thousand times. Wash me yet again from my iniquity, for I have fallen again. Do you spare a sinful person only a set number of times? When Peter asked, "How often will my brother sin against me—shall I forgive him seven times?" You answered, "I say to you not seven times but seventy times seven" [Matt 18:22], counting that finite number for an infinite one. Are you then going to be outdone by a human in forgiveness? Quite the contrary, God is a great Lord and "every living human is total vanity" [Ps 39:5], and God alone is good, but "every man is a liar" [Ps 116:11]. Did you not say: "On any day a sinner moans, 'I shall not remember any of his iniquities'" [Heb 10:17]. See how I, a sinner, am moaning, because "my sores are festering because of my folly. I have become wretched and bent down completely. I seek you in sadness all the day. I am

Rugio a gemitu cordis mei. Domine, ante te omne desiderium
meum; et gemitus meus a te non est absconditus. Cor meum
conturbatum est in me: dereliquit me virtus mea et lumen
oculorum meorum, et ipsum non est mecum." Cur ergo, Domine,
non deles iniquitatem meam? Etsi iam delesti eam secundum
multitudinem miserationum tuarum, amplius lava me ab
iniquitate mea. Adhuc, enim, imperfecte mundatus sum: perfice
opus tuum. Tolle culpam universam; tolle reatum; adauge lumen;
accende cor meum caritate tua; expelle timorem, quia "perfecta
caritas foras mittit timorem." Amor mundi, amor carnis, amor
gloriae, amor proprius prorsus a me recedant. Amplius, et magis
ac magis, lava me ab iniquitate mea, qua contra proximum peccavi;
et a peccato meo, quo Deum offendi, munda me, ut non solum
culpam et reatum, sed etiam peccatorum fomitem deleas. Lava
me, inquam, aqua gratiarum tuarum, "aqua de qua qui biberit
non sitiet in aeternum, sed fiet in eo fons aquae salientis in vita in
aeternam." Lava me aqua lacrimarum mearum; lava me aqua
Scripturarum tuarum, ut inter eos connumerari valeam quibus
dixisti: "Iam vos mundi estis propter sermonem meum."

"Quoniam iniquitatem meam ego cognosco et peccatum
meum contra me est semper."
Quamvis enim ex intuitu misericordiae tuae et miserationum
tuarum, Domine, fiducialiter ad te confugiam, non tamen venio
sicut pharisaeus qui stans apud se orabat, immo se ipsum laudabat
et proximum suum despiciebat, sed sicut publicanus qui nec
audebat ad caelum oculos levare, quoniam iniquitatem meam
ego cognosco. Dum enim peccata mea penso, non audeo sursum
oculos levare, sed cum publicano humiliatus dico: "Deus, propitius
esto mihi peccatori," nam inter spem et metum anima mea

afflicted and utterly cast down. I wail out with sighs from my heart. Lord, my every desire is before you, and my sigh is not hidden from you. My heart is upset within me: my strength has deserted me and even the light of my eyes is not with me" [Ps 38:5-10].

Why then do you not, O Lord, blot out my iniquity? Even if you have blotted it out according to the multitude of your acts of compassion, wash me yet more from my iniquity. For so far I am imperfectly clean; finish your task. Take away all my guilt; take away my penalty; increase my light, set my heart ablaze with your love, cast out fear, because "perfect love casts out fear" [1 John 4:18]. May the love of the world, the love of the flesh, the love of glory, and the love of self utterly depart from me. Wash me again, more and more, from my iniquity by which I have sinned against my neighbor. Cleanse me from my sin by which I have offended God so that you destroy not only my guilt and penalty but also the tinder of sins. Wash me, I say, with the water of your graces, "a water from which those who shall have drunk no longer thirst ever again, but it becomes a fountain in them springing up unto eternal life" [John 4:14]. Wash me with the water of my tears; wash me with the water of your Scriptures so that I may be counted among those to whom you have said, "You are now clean because of my word" [John 15:3].

"Because I ackowledge my iniquity, and my sin is ever before me" [Ps 51:3].

Even though I confidently take refuge in you because of my insight into your mercy and acts of compassion, O Lord, still I do not come like the Pharisee who stood apart and prayed by himself and even praised himself and despised his neighbor but like the publican who did not dare to lift his eyes to heaven, for I acknowledge my own iniquity [Luke 18:9-13]. For when I reflect on my sins, I dare not lift up my eyes but downcast I say with the publican, "God, be merciful to me, a sinner" [Luke

fluctuat, et modo, timore peccatorum quae in me cognosco, despero; modo, spe misericordiae tuae, sublevor. Verum, quia maior est misericordia tua quam miseria mea, semper in te, Domine, sperabo et "misericordias tuas in aeternum cantabo." Scio enim quod non vis mortem peccatoris sed ut convertatur, sed ut iniquitatem suam cognoscat, sed ut peccatum deserat et ad te veniat et vivat. Deus meus, da mihi ut in te vivam, quoniam iniquitatem meam ego cognosco. Scio enim quam gravis sit, quam multa, quam perniciosa. Non ignoro eam ut abscondatur, sed eam ante oculos meos sisto ut lavem eam lacrimis meis et confitear adversum me iniustitiam meam Domino. Nam et peccatum meum, quo superbe contra te egi, contra me est semper: ideo contra me, quia contra te peccavi; vere contra me, quia contra animam meam, quia ante te iudicem semper me accusat, quia semper et ubique me damnat; et adeo contra me, ut sit semper coram me, opponens se mihi ne ad te mea transeat oratio, ut a me tollat misericordiam tuam, ut eam impediat ne ad me transire possit. Ideo contremisco, ideo ingemisco, ideo misericordiam tuam imploro. Sicut ergo, Domine, tu mihi donasti cognoscere iniquitatem meam et flere peccatum meum, ita perfice contritionem meam, imple confessionem meam et perduc ad finem satisfactionem meam. "Omne enim datum optimum et omne donum perfectum desursum est, descendens a te Patre luminum."

"Tibi soli peccavi et malum coram te feci, ut iustificeris in sermonibus tuis et vincas cum iudicaris."
Nimirum tibi soli peccavi, quia mihi praecepisti ut diligerem te propter te, et creaturarum amorem ad te referrem. Ego autem dilexi creaturam magis quam te, diligens eam propter se. Quid

18:13], because my soul tosses between hope and fear, and now I lose heart over the sins which I recognize within me, now I am lifted up in hope of your mercy. But because your mercy is greater than my misery, I will hope in you always, O Lord, and "I shall sing of your mercies forever" [Ps 89:1]. For I know that you do not want the death of the sinner but that he be converted, that he acknowledge his iniquity, turn away from sin and come to you and live.

Grant me, my God, that I may live for you since I acknowledge my iniquity. For I know how serious it is, how manifold, how wicked. I do not ignore it as if it were hidden, but I put it before my eyes so that I may bathe it with my tears and I confess my injustice against myself to the Lord. For before me always is my sin, which I have arrogantly committed against you. It was against myself because I sinned against you. I was against myself because it was against my soul, because it is always accusing me before you, my Judge, because it is condemning me always and everywhere. My sin is so against me that it is always before me, setting itself against me so that my prayer does not reach you, so that it may take your mercy away from me, so that it may hinder your mercy lest it be able to reach unto me. Hence I tremble, hence I sigh, hence I beg your mercy. O Lord, even as you have granted me to acknowledge my iniquity and weep over my sin, so bring to perfection my contrition, make full my confession, and lead my satisfaction to its goal. "For every great gift and every perfect offering is from above, coming down from you, the Father of Lights" [Jas 1:17].

"Against you only have I sinned and done evil before you so that you may be justified in your words and vindicated in your judgment" [Ps 51:4].

Truly I have sinned against you alone, for you have commanded me to love you because of yourself and to trace back the love of creatures to you. But I have loved a creature more than

est autem peccare nisi amore inhaerere creaturae propter se? Quid
autem hoc nisi facere contra te? Certe, qui amat creaturam propter
se, facit creaturam deum suum. Ego itaque tibi soli peccavi, quia
creaturam deum meum constitui; abieci ego te et tibi soli iniuriam
feci. Non enim contra aliquam creaturam peccavi, si finem meum
in creatura constitui, quia non mihi praeceptum fuit ut aliquam
creaturam diligerem propter se. Si enim mihi mandasses ut
angelum solum propter se amarem, et ego pecuniam propter se
dilexissem, utique angelo peccassem; at, cum tu solus diligendus
sis propter te et creatura amanda sit in te et ad te, equidem tibi
soli peccavi quoniam propter se creaturam amavi. Sed quod
deterius est, et malum coram te feci. Non enim erubui peccare
coram te. O Deus, quot peccata commisi coram te, quae nullo
pacto coram hominibus perpetrassem, immo quae nullo modo
homines scire voluissem! Timui magis homines quam te, quia
caecus eram et caecitatem amabam: ideo nec videbam nec
considerabam te. Oculos solum carnis habebam: ideo solum
homines, qui caro sunt, cernebam eosque timebam. Verum tu
omnia peccata mea intuebaris et enumerabas ea: ideo nec ea celare
tibi, nec tergiversari, nec fugere a facie tua potero. "Quo ibo a
Spiritu tuo, et quo a facie tua fugiam?" Quid igitur faciam, et
quo me vertam? Quem inveniam defensorem? quem, obsecro,
nisi te, Deus meus? Quis adeo bonus, quis ita pius, quis tam
misericors, qui pietate omnes creaturas incomprehensibiliter
superas? Tibi enim proprium est misereri semper et parcere, qui
omnipotentiam tuam maxime parcendo et miserando manifestas.
Fateor, Domine, tibi soli peccavi et malum coram te feci. Miserere
mei et omnipotentiam tuam manifesta in me, ut iustificeris in
sermonibus tuis, nam tu dixisti: "Non veni vocare iustos, sed
peccatores ad poenitentiam." Iustificare, Domine, in sermonibus
tuis: voca me, suscipe me, da mihi agere fructum dignum

you, loving it for itself. What is sin, except to love and cling to a creature for its own sake? What is this, except to work against you? Certainly the person who loves a creature for its own sake, make the creatures his god. Therefore I have sinned against you alone, because I set a creature up for my god; I discarded you and have done injury to you alone. I did not sin against a creature if I set up the creature as my end because I was not commanded to love the creature for itself. For if you had ordered me to love only an angel for its own sake, and I had loved money for its own sake, I would indeed have sinned against the angel. But since you alone are to be loved for your own sake and a creature is to be loved in you and for you, I have indeed sinned against you alone because I loved a creature for its own sake. But what is worse, I did evil before you. I was not ashamed to sin before you. O God, how many sins have I committed before you which under no conditions would I have committed before human beings, indeed which I would not in any way want humans to know about! I have feared humans more than you, because I was blind and I loved blindness; hence I neither saw you nor took you into account. I had only fleshly eyes, so I saw only humans, who are flesh, and feared them. But you saw all my sins and kept count of them, so that I will not be able to hide them from you, nor make excuses, nor flee from your face. "Where shall I go away from your Spirit, where shall I flee from your face" [Ps 139:7]? What then shall I do, where shall I turn? Whom shall I find to defend me? Whom, I beg, except you alone, my God? Who is so good, who so kind, who so merciful as you, who incomprehensibly surpasses all creatures in kindness? Always to spare and have mercy is the unique characteristic of you, who display your omnipotence most in sparing and having mercy. I confess, O Lord, that I have sinned against you alone and done evil before you. Take pity on me and display your omnipotence toward me so that you be vindicated in your words, for you have said, "I have not come to call the just but the sinners to repentance" [Luke 5:32]. Do justice to your words, O

poenitentiae: propter hoc enim crucifixus es, propterea mortuus es et sepultus. Dixisti etiam: "Cum exaltatus fuero a terra, omnia traham ad me ipsum." Iustificare in sermonibus tuis: "trahe me; post te curremus in odorem unguentorum tuorum." Dixisti iterum: "Venite ad me omnes qui laboratis et onerati estis, et ego reficiam vos." Ecce venio ad te, onustus peccatis, laborans die ac nocte in gemitu cordis mei. Refice me, Domine, ut iustificeris in sermonibus tuis et vincas cum iudicaris: nam multi dicunt: "Non est salus ipsi in Deo eius"; "Deus dereliquit eum." Vince, Domine, istos, cum ita iudicaris ab eis, ne me derelinquas usquequaque. Da mihi misericordiam et salutem, ut victi sint. Aiunt, enim, quod mei non misereberis, quod me proicies a facie tua, quod me amplius non suscipies. Ita iudicaris ab hominibus; ita de te loquuntur homines; haec sunt eorum iudicia. Sed tu pius, tu misericors, miserere mei et vince eorum iudicia; ostende in me misericordiam tuam; laudetur in me pietas tua; fac me unum de vasis misericordiae tuae, ut iustificeris in sermonibus tuis et vincas cum iudicaris. Te enim homines iudicant rigidum et severum: vince tua pietate et dulcedine iudicium eorum, ut discant homines peccatoribus misereri et accedant delinquentes ad poenitentiam.

"Ecce enim in iniquitatibus conceptus sum, et in peccatis concepit me mater mea."

Ne respicias, Domine, gravitatem peccatorum meorum; ne consideres multitudinem, sed agnosce figmentum tuum: recordare quoniam pulvis sum et omnis caro foenum. Ecce enim in iniquitatibus conceptus sum et in peccatis concepit me mater mea. Mater, inquam, carnalis ex concupiscentia me concepit et in ea peccatum originale contraxi. Quid autem est peccatum

Lord: call me, lift me up, grant me to produce fruit worthy of repentance. This is why you were crucified, why you died and were buried. You also said, "When I shall be lifted up from the earth, I will draw all things to me" [John 12:32]. Do justice to your words: "Draw me; may we hasten after you in the odor of your perfumes" [Cant 1:3]. You also said, "Come to me all you who labor and are heavily burdened, and I will give you rest" [Matt 11:28]. See, I am coming to you, weighed down with sins, laboring day and night with the sighing of my heart. Give me rest, Lord, so that you may be justified in your words and vindicated in your judgment, for many are saying: "He finds no salvation in his God" [Ps 3:2]; "God has forsaken him" [Ps 71:11]. Win out against them, O Lord, so that they may judge that you never desert me. Grant me mercy and salvation so that they may be vanquished. For they say that you will not take pity on me because you will cast me from your face, because you will no longer receive me. Thus do humans pass judgment on you, thus do they talk about you; these are their judgments. But you are kind, you are merciful, take pity on me and overturn their judgments. Show your mercy toward me; may your kindness to me be praised; make me one of the vessels of your mercy so that you may be justified in your words and vindicated in your judgment. Humans regard you as rigid and harsh; overturn their judgment by your kindness and sweetness so that they may learn to take pity on sinners and that the delinquents come forward to repentance.

"Behold, I was conceived in iniquities, and my mother conceived me in sins" [Ps 51:5].

Do not look, O Lord, into the gravity of my sins; do not ponder their number, but recognize your own creation. Call to mind that I am dust and how all flesh is grass. Behold, I was conceived in iniquities, and my mother conceived me in sins. My fleshly mother, I say, conceived me in the concupiscence by which

originale nisi privatio iustitiae originalis et rectitudinis totius
hominis? Ideo homo, conceptus et natus in huiusmodi peccato,
totus obliquus est, totus curvus: "caro concupiscit adversus
spiritum"; ratio debilis est, voluntas infirma; homo fragilis et similis
vanitati: sensus decipiunt eum, imaginatio fallit, ignorantia ducit
eum per invium; infinita habet obstacula quae ipsum a bono
retrahunt et ad malum impellunt. Peccatum, itaque, originale
radix est omnium peccatorum, fomes omnium iniquitatum.
Quamvis, enim, in quolibet homine ex natura sua sit unum,
virtute tamen est omnia peccata. Vides itaque, Domine, quid ego
sum et unde sum: in peccato, enim, originali, quod omnes
iniquitates et omnia peccata continet, conceptus sum, et in eo
concepit me mater mea. In peccatis ego totus natus et laqueis
undique circumdatus, quomodo effugere potero? "Non enim quod
volo hoc ago, sed quod nolo malum hoc facio, quia invenio aliam
legem in membris meis repugnantem legi mentis meae et
captivantem me in lege peccati et mortis." Eo itaque magis pietas
tua me sublevet quo me fragiliorem et tot laqueis circumdatum
intuetur. Quis enim non misereatur infirmo? Quis non
compatiatur languido? Veni, veni, dulcis Samaritane, et
vulneratum semivivum subleva; vulnera mea cura, vinum et oleum
infunde, pone me super iumentum tuum, duc in stabulum,
commenda me stabulario, profer duos denarios et dic ei:
"Quicquid supererogabis, ego, cum rediero, reddam tibi."

"Ecce enim veritatem dilexisti, incerta et occulta sapientiae
tuae manifestasti mihi."
Veni, dulcissime Samaritane! Ecce enim veritatem dilexisti:
veritatem, inquam, promissionum quas humano generi fecisti.
Eas nimirum dilexisti, quia eas fecisti et servasti: nam tuum diligere
ipsum est benefacere. In te ipso, enim, immutabilis es, nec, sicut

I contracted original sin. What is original sin if it is not a privation of original justice and of the uprightness of the whole person? Therefore a human being, conceived and born in this kind of sin is completely twisted, completely bent: "the flesh lusts against the spirit" [Gal 5:17]. His reason is weak, his will is ill; man is fragile and similar to vanity. His senses deceive him, his imagination tricks him, his ignorance leads him astray. He has infinite troubles which drag him from the good and drive him to evil. Original sin is therefore the root of all sins, the tinder of all iniquities. Although by its own nature it is one in any given person, by its power it is all sins. So you see, O Lord, what I am and whence I am. I was conceived in original sin, which contains all iniquities and all sins, and in it my mother conceived me. How can I flee when I was born completely in sins and surrounded by snares on all sides? "I do not do what I want, but it is the evil I do not want which I do because I find another law within my members fighting against the law of my mind and leading me captive in the law of sin and death" [Rom 7: 19-23].

May your kindness therefore uplift me all the more that it sees me all the weaker and surrounded by so many snares. Is there anybody who does not take pity on a sick person? Who does not have compassion for the somebody who is fainting? Come, come, sweet Samaritan, prop me up, for I am half dead from my wounds. Heal my wounds, pour in wine and oil, put me on your beast, lead me to the inn, entrust me to the innkeeper, hand over the two denarii and say to him, "I will repay you for any extra charges you require when I return" [Luke 10:35].

"Behold, you have loved truth, you have revealed to me the uncertain and hidden things of your wisdom" [Ps 51:6].

Come sweet Samaritan! Behold, you have loved truth: the truth, I say, of the promises that you made to the human race. You have indeed loved them because you have made them and kept them, because for you to love is to do good. In yourself you

nos, modo amas modo non amas, ut actus tuae dilectionis transeat et redeat; sed tu es totus amor, qui numquam mutatur. "Deus enim caritas est." Tuum, itaque, diligere creaturam est ei benefacere; et quibus melius facis, hos magis diligis. Quid est, ergo, tuum diligere veritatem nisi facere et servare veritatem? Abrahae promisisti filium cum iam esset senex et Sara sterilis et vetula: promissionem servasti, quia veritatem dilexisti. Filiis Israel terram fluentem lac et mel spopondisti et tandem tradidisti, quia veritatem dilexisti. David pollicitus es, dicens: "De fructu ventris tui ponam super sedem tuam," et factum est, quia veritatem dilexisti. Innumerabiles fuerunt promissiones tuae, in quibus semper fidelis fuisti, quia veritatem dilexisti. Peccatoribus ad te confugientibus veniam et gratiam promisisti, et neminem unquam fraudasti, quia veritatem dilexisti. Filius ille prodigus, qui abiit in regionem longinquam et dissipavit universam substantiam suam vivendo luxuriose, ad se reversus, venit ad te, dicens: "Pater, peccavi in caelum et coram te; iam non sum dignus vocari filius tuus; fac me sicut unum de mercenariis tuis." Cum adhuc longe esset, oculis tuae pietatis eum intuitus es: occurristi ei; cecidisti super collum eius, et osculatus es eum; protulisti stolam primam; anulum in manu eius et calciamenta in pedibus eius posuisti; vitulum saginatum occidisti; totam domum laetificasti, dicens: "Laetemur et epulemur, quia hic filius meus mortuus erat et revixit; perierat et inventus est." Cur haec, Domine Deus? Nempe quia veritatem dilexisti. Dilige ergo, Pater misericordiarum, hanc veritatem in me, qui ad te revertor de regione longinqua. Occurre mihi et osculum tui oris da; redde prima ornamenta; trahe me in domum tuam; occide vitulum saginatum, ut in me laetentur omnes qui sperant in te, et pariter convivemur in conviviis spiritualibus.

are unchanging; unlike us, you do not love one moment and stop loving the next, as if your act of loving comes and goes. But you are total love, which never changes. "God is love" [1 John 4:16]. For you to love a creature is to do good to it, and you love more those whom you treat better. What then does loving truth mean for you if not doing and preserving the truth? You promised Abraham a son when he was already an old man and his wife Sarah was aged and sterile. You kept your promise because you loved truth. You pledged to the children of Israel a land flowing with milk and honey and eventually you gave them it because you loved truth. You made a promise to David, saying: "I will put on your throne one from the fruit of your loins" [Ps 132:11], and it took place because you loved truth. Countless were your promises, to which you were always faithful because you loved truth. You promised pardon and grace to sinners who took refuge in you, and you never cheated anyone because you loved truth.

The prodigal son, who went off to a distant land and dissipated all his belongings in living riotously, having reexamined himself came to you and said, "Father, I have sinned against heaven before you; I am no longer worthy to be called your son; make me like one of your hired hands" [Luke 15:19-24]. When he was still far off you spotted him with your eyes of kindness, you ran to him, you fell upon his shoulders and kissed him; you brought out the best robe and put a ring on his hand and shoes on his feet; you slew the fatted calf; you made joyous the whole household and said, "Let us make merry and feast, for this son of mine was dead and lives again; he was lost and is found" [Luke 15:22-24].

Why did you do this, O Lord God? Precisely because you loved truth. Then, O Father of mercies, love this truth in my case, for I am returning to you from a distant land. Run to me and give me a kiss with your mouth; hand me the best clothing, escort me into your home; kill the fatted calf so that all who hope in you may take joy in me, and we may feast together in spiritual

Num, Domine, mihi soli non custodies hanc veritatem? "Si
iniquitates observaveris, Domine, Domine, quis sustinebit?"
Equidem tu non observabis iniquitates, quia veritatem dilexisti:
dilexisti quidem immenso amore. Quae namque est veritas quam
dilexisti? Nonne Filius tuus, qui dixit: "Ego sum via, veritas et
vita"? Ipse enim est veritas a qua omnis veritas in caelo et in terra
nominatur. Hanc igitur dilexisti, et in ea sola tibi complacuisti.
Et quid est quod in ea sola tibi complacuisti? Quia eam solam
sine macula invenisti, et pro peccatoribus eam mori voluisti.
Custodi ergo, Deus, hanc veritatem. Ecce ego peccator magnus,
in quo tu custodias eam, cui tu indulgeas peccata multa, quem
sanguine Christi tui abluas, quem per passionem eius redimas.
Cur, Domine, hanc de Filio tuo notitiam? Cur hanc de eo fidem
tradidisti mihi? Num ut maiori afficiar dolore, videns
redemptionem meam et minime attingens eam? Absit: sed, ut
intelligens mihi paratam veniam, apprehendam illam per Christi
gratiam. Redime ergo me, Domine, nam incerta et occulta
sapientiae tuae manifestasti mihi, ut haec ipsa cognitio me adiuvet
et ad salutem perducat. Haec profecto non cognoverunt
philosophi; haec fuerunt eis incerta; haec erant eis penitus occulta;
haec ante incarnationem Filii tui, exceptis paucis quos tu dilexisti,
nullus hominum cognovit. Scrutatores orbis curiosissimi, sapientes
dico huius saeculi, trans caelum oculos levaverunt et hanc tuam
sapientiam invenire non potuerunt, "quia abscondisti haec a
sapientibus et prudentibus, et revelasti ea parvulis," idest humilibus
piscatoribus et sanctis prophetis tuis, qui ea nobis tradiderunt. Si
ergo incerta et occulta sapientiae tuae Scripturarumque tuarum
manifestasti mihi, cur frustra ea cognosco? Frustra autem cognosco
illa, si me ad salutem non perducunt. Nam et philosophi, "cum

banquets. Is it only toward me that you do not observe this truth: "If you keep track of iniquities, Lord, Lord, who will bear it" [Ps 130:3]? You do not keep track of iniquities because you have loved truth; you have indeed loved with a boundless love. What is the truth that you have loved? Is it not what your Son said, "I am the way, the truth, and the life" [John 14:6]? For he himself is the truth from which all truth in heaven and on earth gets its name. So it is this truth that you have loved, and in it alone you have taken pleasure. What does it mean, that you have taken pleasure in it alone? Because it is only this truth that you have found without flaw and you wished this Truth to die for sinners. Guard then, O God, this truth. See, I am a great sinner in whom you guard this truth, whom you have forgiven many sins, whom you wash in the blood of your Christ, whom you redeem by his passion. O Lord, why do I have this knowledge about your Son? Why have you handed over to me this faith about him? Is it so that I may be afflicted by greater pain when I see my redemption and cannot touch it? On the contrary: rather that by understanding the redemption prepared for me, I may attain it by the grace of Christ. Redeem me, Lord, for you have revealed to me the uncertain and hidden things of your wisdom so that this very knowledge may help me and lead me to salvation.

These things the philosophers did not really recognize; these were uncertain to them; these were totally hidden from them; no human being, except for a few whom you loved, knew these things before the incarnation of your Son. Those who studied the earth with deep curiosity—I mean the wise of this world—lifted their eyes across the sky and were not able to find this wisdom of yours, "because you have hidden these things from the wise and clever and revealed them to babes" [Matt 11:25], that is to lowly fishermen and to your holy prophets, who have handed them down to us. If you have revealed to me the uncertain and hidden things of your wisdom and your Scriptures, why do I understand them to no purpose? I understand them to no purpose if they do not lead

cognovissent Deum, non sicut Deum glorificaverunt aut gratias egerunt, sed evanuerunt in cogitationibus suis dicentes enim se esse sapientes, stulti facti sunt." Num de numero istorum me esse patieris? Absit. Tu es enim ipsa misericordia, quae nunquam poenitentes deserit. Parce ergo, Domine; parce famulo tuo, et iube ipsum esse in numero parvulorum tuorum, ut incerta et occulta sapientiae tuae, quae manifestasti ei, ducant eum ad fontem sapientiae quae est in excelsis, ut lauderis in opere misericordiae tuae quam feceris cum servo tuo, Domine, qui nunquam deseris sperantes in te.

"Asperges me, Domine, hyssopo, et mundabor; lavabis me et super nivem dealbabor."

Quia, Domine, veritatem dilexisti, et incerta et occulta sapientiae tuae manifestasti mihi, spem magnam concepi, et confido quod non repelles me a facie tua, sed asperges me hyssopo, et mundabor. Hyssopus est herba humilis, calida et odorifera, quae quid aliud significat quam Filium tuum Dominum nostrum Iesum Christum, "qui humiliavit semetipsum usque ad mortem, mortem autem crucis," qui calore suae immensae caritatis "dilexit nos et lavit nos a peccatis nostris in sanguine suo," qui odore bonitatis et mansuetudinis suae atque iustitiae totum mundum suavitate replevit? Hoc ergo hyssopo asperges me quando virtutem sanguinis eius effundes super me, quando per fidem habitabit Christus in me, quando per dilectionem ei coniunctus fuero, quando humilitatem eius et passionem imitabor. Tunc mundabor ab omnibus immunditiis meis; tunc lavabis me lacrimis meis a Christi amore fluentibus. "Tunc laborabo in gemitu meo; lavabo per singulas noctes lectum meum; lacrimis meis stratum meum rigabo." Tunc ergo lavabis me et super nivem dealbabor.

me to salvation. For the philosophers also "although they knew God, did not glorify him as God or give him thanks, but became vain in their thoughts; for in claiming to be wise, they became fools" [Rom 1:21-22]. Will you allow me to be among their number? Not at all. For you are mercy itself, who never deserts the penitent. Spare, O Lord, spare your servant, and command that he be counted among your little ones so that the uncertain and secret things of your wisdom, which you have revealed to him, may lead him to the fountain of wisdom which is in heaven above so that you may be praised in the work of your mercy which you have performed for your servant, O Lord, who never desert those who hope in you.

"You will sprinkle me with hyssop, and I shall be made clean and become whiter than snow" [Ps 51:7].

O Lord, because you have loved the truth and have revealed to me the uncertain and hidden things of your wisdom, I have conceived a great hope and am confident that you will not cast me away from your face but will sprinkle me with hyssop, and I shall be made clean. Hyssop is a lowly plant, warm and sweet-smelling. What else does it signify but your Son, our Lord, Jesus Christ, "who humbled himself unto death, even the death of the cross" [Phil 2:8], who in the warmth of his boundless charity "loved us and washed us from our sins in his own blood" [Rev 1:5], who filled the whole world with the odor of his goodness and gentleness and with the sweetness of his justice? You will sprinkle me then with this hyssop when you will pour over me the power of his blood, when Christ will dwell through faith within me, when I will be joined to him in love, when I will imitate his humility and passion. Then will I be cleansed of all my impurities; then will you wash me with my tears that flow because of the love of Christ. "Then will I grow weary with my moaning; every night will I wash my bed and drench my couch with my tears" [Ps 6:6]. Then you will wash me and I shall be-

Nix enim candida est et frigida. Ita profecto, Domine, si me hyssopo asperseris, super nivem dealbabor; quia tua maxima luce perfundar, quae omnem corporalem superat candorem, et per eam, amore caelestium bonorum accensus, omnes carnis affectus relinquam: frigidus ad terrena et ad caelestia inflammatus.

"Auditui meo dabis gaudium et laetitiam; et exultabunt ossa humiliata."

Tunc enim, Domine, orabo ad te. "Mane," idest in initio lucis tuae, "exaudies vocem meam, audiamque quid loquatur in me Dominus Deus, quoniam loquetur pacem in plebem suam"; dabisque mihi pacem, Domine: pacem dabis mihi, quia in te speravi. Auditui meo dabis gaudium et laetitiam, cum audiam quod audivit Maria. Et quid audivit Maria? De illa loquor, quae flevit secus pedes tuos. Quid igitur haec audivit? "Fides tua te salvam fecit: vade in pace." Audiam quoque quod audivit latro: "Hodie mecum eris in Paradiso." Gaudium itaque mihi erit de remissione peccatorum, laetitia de promissione bonorum. Numquid non gaudebo et non laetabor quando reddes mihi "duplicia pro omnibus peccatis meis?" Tunc gustare incipiam quam dulcis est Dominus; tunc discam in caelestibus habitare; tunc dicam cum Propheta: "Quam magna multitudo dulcedinis tuae, Domine, quam abscondisti timentibus te." Tunc gaudebo et laetabor, et exultabunt ossa humiliata. Quid sunt ossa, quae carnem sustinent, nisi animae rationalis vires, quae carnis nostrae fragilitatem portant, ne in omnia vitia fluat, ne totus homo efficiatur caro, penitusque tabescat? Ossa ergo haec humiliata sunt quia nimis debilitata est ratio, et voluntas ad malum valde prona. Iam, iam non caro oboedit rationi, sed ratio carni! Vitiis resistere

come whiter than snow. Snow is white and cold. Lord, if you shall have indeed sprinkled me with hyssop, I shall be whiter than snow because I will be steeped in your enormous light which surpasses all bodily whiteness and through it, set ablaze with the love of heavenly goods, I will leave behind all the affections for the flesh, I will be cold toward the things of earth and set afire for the things of heaven.

"You will give joy and gladness to my hearing; the bones you have broken will rejoice" [Ps 51:8].

"For then, O Lord, will I pray to you. In the morning" (that is at the beginning of your light) "you will hear my voice" [Ps 5:3], "and I will hear what the Lord God is saying to me, for he speaks of peace for his people" [Ps 85:8]; and you will give me peace, O Lord. You will give me peace because I have hoped in you. You will give joy and gladness to my hearing since I will hear what Mary heard. What did Mary hear? I speak of her who wept at your feet. What then did she hear? "Your faith has saved you, go in peace" [Luke 7:50]. I will hear also what the thief heard: "This day you will be with me in paradise" [Luke 23:43]. My joy will come from the remission of my sins, my rejoicing from your promise of good things. Should I not rejoice and not be glad when you render me "double for all my sins" [Isa 40:2]? Then shall I begin to taste how sweet the Lord is; then shall I learn to dwell in heavenly places; then shall I say with the Prophet, "How great is your sweetness, O Lord, which you have reserved for those who fear you" [Ps 31:19]. Then shall I rejoice and be glad and the bones you have broken will rejoice. What are the bones which hold up our flesh except the powers of our rational soul which carry the fragility of our flesh lest it gush out into all sorts of vices, lest the whole human being become flesh and completely waste away? These bones then are broken because our reason is too weak and our will is much inclined toward evil. Now, now our flesh does not obey our reason, but our reason obeys the

non possum, quia ossa mea humiliata sunt. Et quare humiliata? Quia "reliquerunt te fontem aquae vivae et foderunt sibi cisternas dissipatas quae continere non valent aquas," quia gratia tua non sunt repletae, sine qua nemo potest bene vivere. Sine te, enim, nihil possumus facere. Confidebant in virtute sua, quae non erat virtus: ideo defecerunt in stultitia sua. Veniat ergo virtus tua, Domine, et exultabunt ossa humiliata. Veniat gratia tua; veniat fides, quae per dilectionem operatur; veniant virtutes et dona, et exultabunt ossa humiliata. Exultabit quippe ratio, laetabitur memoria, gaudebit voluntas: nimirum exultabunt, quia extra se salient dum ad bona opera prodibunt; virtute magna exercebuntur in eis, nec deficient; sed, te adiuvante, ad finem usque se perducent.

"Averte faciem tuam a peccatis meis, et omnes iniquitates meas dele."

Cur, Domine, respicis peccata mea? Cur numeras ea? Cur adeo diligenter consideras? Numquid nescis quia homo tamquam flos agri? Cur non respicis potius in faciem Christi tui? Heu me miserum! Cur video te mihi iratum? Peccavi, fateor, sed tu benignus miserere mei. Averte faciem tuam a peccatis meis. Facies tua cognitio tua est. Averte, itaque, cognitionem tuam a peccatis meis. Non loquor de cognitione simplicis apprehensionis, qua omnia semper vides, sed de cognitione approbationis et reprobationis, qua opera iustorum approbas et peccata impiorum reprobando condemnas. Noli mea peccata ita cognoscere ut mihi imputes ea, sed averte faciem tuam a peccatis meis ut per misericordiam tuam deleantur. Respice, Domine, animam quam creasti; respice imaginem tuam quam formasti. Tu enim creasti eam ad imaginem tuam, et ego miser superinduxi imaginem

flesh. I cannot resist my vices because my bones have been broken. Why broken? Because "they have left you the fountain of living water and dug for themselves broken cisterns which cannot hold water" [Jer 2:13], because they are not filled with your grace, without which nobody can live an upright life. Without you we can do nothing. They kept trusting in their own strength, but it was not strength, so they failed in their own folly. So let your strength come, O Lord, and the broken bones will rejoice. Let your grace come, let the faith come which works through love; let strength and gifts come, and the broken bones will rejoice. Reason shall exult, memory shall rejoice, the will shall be glad: they will indeed exult because they leap beyond themselves when they overflow into good works. They will work at them with great strength, nor will they grow weak, but with you helping them they shall carry on right to the end.

"Turn your face away from my sins, and blot out all my iniquities" [Ps 51:9].

Why, O Lord, do you look upon my sins? Why do you keep count of them? Why do you ponder them so carefully? Do you not know that a human being is like the flower of the field? Why not rather look upon the face of your Christ? Alas for wretched me! Why do I see you so angry with me? I have sinned—I admit it—but have mercy on me in your kindness. Turn your face away from my sins. Your face is your knowledge. Turn then your knowledge away from my sins. I speak not of the knowledge of simple apprehension, by which you are always seeing all things, but of the knowledge of approval and disapproval, by which you approve the works of the just and by your disapproval you condemn the sins of the wicked. Do not so know my sins that you impute them against me, but turn away your face from my sins so that they may be blotted out through your mercy. Lord, look upon the soul you have created, look upon your image which you have fashioned. You created it in your own image, and I in

diaboli. Averte, Domine, faciem tuam ab imagine diaboli ut non
irascaris mihi, et respice imaginem tuam ut miserearis mei, o
misericors Domine. Recordare quia Zacchaeum ascendentem in
arborem sycomorum respexisti, et in domum eius descendisti?
Quod plane nunquam fecisses, si imaginem diaboli in eo
respexisses; sed quia imaginem tuam in eo vidisti, compassus es
ei, et salutem ei tribuisti. Ipse male ablata restituere quadruplicata
et dimidium bonorum suorum pauperibus erogare promisit, et
consecutus est misericordiam et salutem. Ego me totum trado
tibi; nihil mihi reservo; tibi semper servire sincero corde promitto.
Vota mea reddam omnibus diebus vitae meae. Cur ergo, Domine,
in me quoque non respicis imaginem tuam? Ut quid adhinc
peccata mea consideras? Averte, obsecro, faciem tuam a peccatis
meis et omnes iniquitates meas dele. Omnes, rogo, dele ut nulla
remaneat. Scriptum est enim: "Qui totam legem servaverit, in
uno autem offenderit, factus est omnium reus," idest factus est
reus Gehennae, quae est poena omnium peccatorum quae ducunt
ad mortem. Dele, ergo, omnes iniquitates meas, ne ulla te offendat
quae me omnium reum faciat.

"Cor mundum crea in me, Deus, et spiritum rectum innova
in visceribus meis."

Nam cor meum dereliquit me, nunquam de me cogitat. Suae
salutis penitus oblitum, per devia vagatur, peregre profectum est,
sequitur vanitates, et oculi eius in finibus terrae. Vocavi eum et
non respondit mihi; abiit et periit; in peccatis venundatum est.
Quid ergo, Domine, quid dicam? Cor mundum crea in me, Deus:
cor humile, cor mansuetum, cor pacificum, cor benignum, cor
pium, quod nulli inferat malum, quod malum pro malo non
reddat, sed pro malo bonum; quod te super omnia diligat, te
semper cogitet, de te loquatur, tibi gratias agat, in hymnis et

my misery have superimposed the image of the Devil. Turn, O Lord, your face away from the image of the Devil so that you do not become angry at me, and look upon your own image so that you may have mercy on me, O merciful Lord.

Do you remember how you looked upon Zacchaeus climbing up the sycamore tree and how you went down to his home? Obviously you would never have done that if you had seen the image of the Devil in him. But because you saw your own image in him, you had compassion on him and granted him salvation. He promised to restore fourfold what he had taken wrongfully and to set aside half of his goods for the poor, and he attained mercy and salvation. I give you my whole self; I keep back nothing for myself; I promise to serve you forever with a sincere heart. I shall fulfill my vows all the days of my life. Why then, Lord, do you not look upon your image in me? Why do you still keep in mind my sins? Turn your face away from my sins, I beg you, and blot out all my iniquities. I ask you to blot them all out so that not one remains. For it is written: "The person who observes the whole law but offends on one point becomes guilty of it all" [Jas 2:10], that is, he becomes guilty of Hell, which is the punishment of all the sins which lead to death. So blot out all my iniquities lest any offend you and make me guilty of them all.

"Create a clean heart in me, O God, and renew a right spirit within me" [Ps 51:10].

My heart deserts me, it never thinks about me. Utterly forgetful of its salvation, it goes astray; it has set out for foreign lands, it chases after vanities, and its eyes are on the ends of the earth. I called to my heart, and it did not answer me; it went out and died; it has been put up for sale in its sins. What then, Lord, what can I say? Create a clean heart in me, O God; a humble heart, a gentle heart, a peaceful heart, a kind heart, a devout heart which brings harm on no one, which does not pay back evil with evil but good for evil; which loves you above all things, constantly

canticis spiritualibus delectetur, in caelis conversetur. Cor tale crea
in me, Deus; et ex nihilo produc illud, ut quale non potest esse
per naturam, fiat tale per gratiam. Haec enim a te solo per
creationem in animam venit; haec est forma cordis mundi; haec
omnes virtutes secum trahens, omnia vitia pariter expellit. Cor
itaque mundum per gratiam tuam crea in me, Deus, et spiritum
rectum innova in visceribus meis. "Spiritus enim tuus deducet
me in viam rectam," quia me a terrenis affectibus purgabit et ad
caelestia sublevabit. Amans enim et amatum sunt unum. Qui
ergo amat corpora, corpus est; qui vero spiritum diligit, spiritus
est. Da mihi spiritum te amantem, teque summum spiritum
adorantem. "Nam spiritus est Deus, et eos, qui adorant eum, in
spiritu et veritate, oportet adorare." Da spiritum rectum, non
quae sua sed quae tua sunt quaerentem. Innova spiritum rectum
in visceribus meis; innova, quia primum, quem mihi dederas,
peccata mea extinxerunt. Da spiritum novum, qui innovet quod
inveteratum est. Nam anima mea spiritus est, et a te ita creata ut
in se recta sit. Ex natura, enim, sua te super se amat, et propter te
omnia desiderat: nam amor naturalis rectus est eo quod a te est,
sed ex prava voluntate sua in peccatis inveterata est, et amorem
naturalem contabescere fecit. Innova ergo hunc spiritum et hunc
amorem per gratiam tuam, ut recte incedat secundum naturam
suam. Innova in visceribus meis, ut intus radices ita firment ut
nunquam amplius possit evelli. Innova, inquam, in visceribus
meis, ut semper amore caelesti me urat, semper me faciat ad te
suspirare, te iugiter amplecti et nunquam deserere.

"Ne proicias me a facie tua, et Spiritum Sanctum tuum ne
auferas a me."

Ecce, Domine, sto ante faciem tuam ut inveniam misericordiam tuam. Sto ante bonitatem et benignitatem tuam. Expecto

thinks of you, speaks about you, gives you thanks, delights in hymns and spiritual songs, whose citizenship is in heaven. Create that sort of heart in me, O God. Create it from nothing so that what cannot exist as such from nature may be made such by grace. Grace comes into the soul through creation by you alone; grace is the form of a clean heart; grace draws along with it all the virtues and likewise casts out all vices. Through your grace, then, create a clean heart in me, O God, and renew an upright spirit within me. "May your spirit lead me along the right path" [Ps 143:10], because it will purge me of earthly inclinations and lift me up to heavenly ones. The lover and the beloved are one. The person who loves bodies is a body; the one who loves the spirit is spirit. Give me a spirit that loves you, a supreme spirit that adores you. "For God is spirit, and those who adore him should adore him in spirit and truth" [John 4:24]. Give an upright spirit which seeks not things which are its own but which are yours. Renew an upright spirit within me; renew it, because my sins have killed off the first spirit which you gave me. Give a new spirit which may renew what has grown old. My soul is a spirit, and you created it so that it would be right in itself. By its own nature it loved you above itself and desired everything for your sake. For natural love is upright in so far as it is from you, but it has grown old in sins from its depraved will and has caused its natural love to waste away. Renew this spirit and this love by your grace so that it may walk straight according to its nature. Renew it within me so that its roots may grow so strong within that they can never more be pulled out. Renew it within me, I say, so that it may burn me with a heavenly love, make me always pant after you, always embrace you, and never desert you.

"Do not cast me from your face, and take not your Holy Spirit from me" [Ps 51:11].

Behold, O Lord, I stand before your face so that I may find your mercy. I stand before your goodness and kindness. I wait for

gratam responsionem tuam: ne proicias me a facie tua confusum. Quis unquam, Domine, venit ad te et confusus abscessit? Quis rogavit faciem tuam et vacuus abiit? Certe, abundantia pietatis tuae et merita supplicum excellis et vota, pluraque praestas quam homines desiderare aut intelligere possunt. A saeculo non est auditum quod venientem ad te proieceris a facie tua confusum. Numquid, Domine, primus ero a facie tua proiectus? An a me vis initium habere confundendi venientem ad te? Num amplius non vis misereri et parcere? Absit. Chananaea te sequebatur; clamabat; vocibus aera implebat; discipulos tuos ad compassionem provocabat, et tu tacebas. Ipsa perseverabat pulsans; te adorabat, dicens: "Domine, adiuva me," et tu nec respondebas. Discipuli rogaverunt pro ea, dicentes: "Dimitte eam, quia clamat post nos." Quid, obsecro, quid, Domine, eis respondisti? Equidem quod inaniter flebat, quod frustra laborabat. Dixisti enim: "Non sum missus nisi ad oves quae perierunt domus Israel." Quid, hoc audito, debuit Chananaea facere? Utique de gratia, quam desiderabat, desperare. Nec tamen desperavit, sed, confidens de tua misericordia, iterum atque iterum rogabat, dicens: "Domine, adiuva me." Cui importune insistenti, "Domine," respondisti: "Non est bonum tollere panem filiorum et mittere canibus," ac si patenter dixisses: "Recede a me. Vos Chananaei canes estis, immundi estis, idolatrae estis; dona gratiarum caelestium ad vos non pertinent: non debeo ea tollere Judaeis Deum verum colentibus et dare vobis canibus, daemones adorantibus." Quid nunc facies, o Chananaea? Erubesce iam et recede, quia iratus est Dominus non solum tibi sed universae genti tuae. Quis, Domine Deus, ad haec tua verba confusus non recessisset? quis non submurmurasset? quis non te crudelem iudicasset? Et tamen haec

your gracious response; do not drive me from your face in shame. Who, O Lord, ever came to you and went away in shame? Who sought your face and went off empty-handed? Certainly the abundance of your kindness exceeds the merits and prayers of your suppliants, and you grant more than humans are able to desire or know. Not for ages has it been heard that you have driven off from your face in shame somebody who came to you. Will I be the first, O Lord, to be cast away from your face? Do you want to make a start with me of confounding those who come to you? Do you want no longer to have mercy and to spare? Quite the contrary.

The Canaanite woman followed you, she called out, she filled the air with her cries. She provoked your disciples to compassion, and you kept quiet. She kept on knocking, she worshiped you and said, "Lord, help me," and you did not answer her. The disciples interceded for her and said, "Dismiss her, for she is shouting after us." What, I beg you, Lord, what did you reply to them? That she was weeping to no purpose, that she was laboring in vain. You said, "I am not sent except to the sheep who have perished from the house of Israel." What was the Canaanite woman to do when she heard this? Obviously to despair of the grace she desired. But she did not despair but confident of your mercy again and again kept asking and saying, "Lord, help me." Lord, you replied to her when she insisted importunately, "It is not right to take the bread of the children and throw it to dogs," just as if you had clearly said, "Get away from me. You Canaanites are dogs, you are unclean, you are idol worshipers, the gifts of heavenly graces are not for you. I should not take them from the Jews who worship the true God and give them to you dogs who worship demons." Now what are you going to do, O Canaanite woman? Blush now with shame and get out of the way, because the Lord is angry not only at you but at all your nation. Who, O Lord God, would not retreat in embarrassment at these words of yours? Who would not grumble? Who would not think you cruel?

ipsa mulier in oratione perstitit; spem non dimisit; verba dura non aegre tulit; non irata est; sed magis humiliata, in petitione persistens, confidenter dixit etiam: "Domine, verum est quod dicis, sed panem non peto, gratias filiorum non postulo, quia catula ego sum. Micas peto quae cadunt de mensa filiorum tuorum: ipsi enim miraculis et gratiis abundent. Mihi autem haec minima gratia non negetur, ut filia mea a daemonio liberetur, 'nam et catelli edunt de micis quae cadunt de mensa dominorum suorum.'" Ecce, quanta fides! quanta fiducia! quanta humilitas! Ideo tu non iratus de tanta importunitate, sed gavisus de eius virtute, dixisti: "Mulier, magna est fides tua: fiat tibi sicut vis." Cur haec scripta sunt, Domine Deus? Ut discamus in te sperare et ut in oratione pie et humiliter perseveremus, quia dare vis. Sed "regnum caelorum vim patitur et violenti rapiunt illum." "Quaecumque, enim, scripta sunt, ad nostram doctrinam scripta sunt, ut per patientiam et consolationem Scripturarum spem habeamus." Ne ergo proicias me a facie tua, Domine, qui die noctuque ante faciem tuam deflens et humilis sto, non ut me liberes a daemonis oppressione corporali, sed ut animam meam eripias ab eius potestate spirituali. Ne me confundas, bone Iesu, quia in te solo spero. Non est mihi salus nisi in te, Domine. Omnes, enim, dereliquerunt me: nam et fratres et filii mei abiecerunt me: viscera mea abominantur me; neminem amplius habeo adiutorem praeter te. Ne ergo proicias me a facie tua, et Spiritum Sanctum tuum ne auferas a me. "Nemo potest dicere: 'Dominus Jesus,' nisi in Spiritu Sancto." Itaque, si ego invoco te, Domine Iesu, hoc facio in Spiritu Sancto. Si de peccatis commissis doleo, si veniam peto, hoc certe facio in Spiritu Sancto. Ideo te obsecro Spiritum Sanctum tuum ne auferas a me, ut mecum sit

Still this same woman persevered in her prayer; she did not lose hope; she did not become bitter over your harsh words; she did not become angry. Despite her greater humiliation, she kept up her demand and even said with confidence, "Lord, what you say is true, but I am not asking for bread, I am not seeking the favors given to your children, for I am only a puppy. I am asking for the crumbs that fall from the table of your children. May they abound in miracles and favors. But don't deny me this tiny favor, that my daughter be freed from a demon, 'for even the puppies eat from the crumbs that fall from the table of their lords.'" Notice how much faith she has! How much trust! How much humility! So you were not angered by such brashness, but delighted with her virtue you said, "Woman, great is your faith. May what you want happen to you" [Matt 15:22-28].

Why were these things written, Lord God? So that we might learn to hope in you and devoutly and humbly persevere in prayer because you want to give. "The kingdom of heaven suffers violence, and the violent carry it away" [Matt 11:12]. "Everything that has been written has been written to teach us so that we may have hope through patience and the consolation of the Scriptures" [Rom 15:4]. Do not then drive me away from your face, O Lord. Day and night I stand weeping and humble before your face, not so that you may free me from the bodily oppression of the demon but so that you may deliver my soul from his spiritual power. Good Jesus, do not put me to shame, for I hope in you alone. There is no salvation for me, except in you, O Lord. Everybody has deserted me, for my brothers and sons have cast me off. My own inner organs hate me. I no longer have any helper except you. Do not then drive me away from your face, and do not take your Holy Spirit away from me. "No one can say 'Jesus is Lord' except in the Holy Spirit" [1 Cor 12:3]. If therefore I call upon you, Lord Jesus, I do it in the Holy Spirit. If I am pained by the sins I have committed, if I seek pardon, I certainly do it in the Holy Spirit. So I beg you not to take your Holy Spirit away from

et mecum laboret. "Nam quid oremus, ut oportet, nescimus; sed Spiritus" adiuvat infirmitatem nostram et "postulat pro nobis," idest postulare nos facit, "gemitibus inenarrabilibus." Ne ergo Spiritum Sanctum tuum auferas a me, ut me orare doceat et in labore me adiuvet, faciatque me in orationibus et lacrimis persistere, ut tandem inveniam gratiam coram te et serviam tibi omnibus diebus vitae meae.

"Redde mihi laetitiam salutaris tui, et spiritu principali confirma me."

Rem magnam peto, Domine: "quoniam tu, Deus, magnus Dominus et rex magnus super omnes Deos." Tibi iniuriam facit qui a te parva petit. Parva sunt omnia quae transeunt; parva omnia corporalia, magna et pretiosa spiritualia. Tolle spiritum; tolle animam a corpore: quid remanet nisi stercus, quid nisi pulvis et umbra? Ergo tantum distat inter spiritum et corpus, quantum inter corpus et umbram eius. Qui igitur petit a te corporea, parva petit; qui vero spiritualia, magna profecto postulat, maxima autem qui tui salutaris laetitiam petit. Quid est enim salutare tuum, nisi Iesus filius tuus? Hic est verus Deus et vita aeterna. Cur ergo a te Patre immenso liberalissimo hoc salutare non petam, quem pro me super lignum tradidisti? Tu eum mihi obtulisti: quare petere ipsum erubescam? Maximum et infinitum munus est: non sum ego tanto munere dignus. Te tamen decet tam magna munera donare. Propter hanc itaque ineffabilem pietatem audeo ad te fiducialiter accedere, et salutaris tui laetitiam petere. "Nam si a patre carnis suae petierit quispiam filius piscem, numquid porriget ei serpentem? et si petierit ovum numquid dabit ei scorpionem? et si petierit panem, numquid dabit ei lapidem?" Si ergo patres

me, that he may be with me and work with me. "We do not know how to pray as we ought, but the Spirit" helps our weakness and "petitions for us with groans that surpass words" [Rom 8:26], that is, he makes us petition. So do not take your Holy Spirit away from me, so that he can teach me to pray and help me in my work and make me persevere in my prayers and tears so that I may finally find grace before you and serve you all the days of my life.

"Give me back the joy of your salvation, and make strong in me a willing spirit" [Ps 51:12].

Lord, I am asking for something great: "For you, God, are a great Lord and a great King above all the gods" [Ps 95:3]. The person who asks you for little things does you an injustice. Everything that passes away is little; all corporeal things are little, and spiritual things are great and precious. Take away the spirit, take the soul out of the body; what remains except dung, what except dust and shadow? For the disparity between spirit and body is as great as that between a body and its shadow. The person who requests physical objects from you requests little things, but the person who asks for things spiritual is indeed after something great. But the greatest gifts go to the person who asks for the joy of your salvation. What is your salvation except your Son Jesus? He is true God and eternal life. Why then do I not beg from you, most rich and most generous Father, for this salvation, whom you handed over for me on the wood [of the cross]? You offered him up for me; why should I be ashamed to ask for him? He is the supreme and infinite gift. I am not worthy of such a gift. But it is fitting for you to give such great gifts. Because of this ineffable kindness, therefore, I dare to approach you with confidence and request the joy of your salvation.

"If some son were to ask his human father for a fish, would he offer him a serpent? If he were to ask for an egg, would he give him a scorpion? If he were to ask for bread, would he give him a

carnales, cum sint mali et peccatores, volunt bona eis a te data dare filiis suis, quanto magis tu, Pater caelestis, qui per essentiam bonus es, dabis Spiritum bonum petenti te? Ecce filius tuus, de regione longinqua reversus, dolens et poenitens petit a te piscem fidei. Sicut enim piscis latitat sub aquis, ita fides est de his quae non videntur. Petit, dico, fidem veram, ut laetetur in salutari tuo. Numquid porriges ei serpentem? Numquid dabis ei infidelitatis venena a tortuoso et antiquo serpente diabolo proficiscentia? Peto a te, Domine, ovum spei, ut sicut ex ovo speratur pullus, ita ex spe ad visionem salutaris tui mihi venire concedas, ut de ipsa spe egrediatur visio, quasi pullus de ovo. Peto ovum spei, ut interim spe ipsa sublevetur anima mea in hac lacrimarum valle, et laetetur in salutari tuo. Numquid dabis mihi desperationis scorpionem, ut sicut scorpio in extremitate caudae habet venenum, ita et ego in extremo vitae meae reservem peccatum, blandiarque mihi in illecebris mundi, sicut scorpio in facie blandus videtur? Peto etiam a te panem caritatis Christi, qua se sicut panis omnibus communicat, ut semper gaudeam in salutari tuo. Numquid lapidem dabis mihi: hoc est cordis duritiam? Absit. Cur itaque diffidam petere et impetrare magna a te, Domine, qui me excitas et invitas ad petendum et pulsandum usque ad importunitatem? Quid vero tibi gratum magis et mihi salubrius petere possum, quam ut reddas mihi laetitiam salutaris tui? Iam gustavi quam dulcis sit Dominus, quam leve et suave sit onus eius. Memor sum quanta pace, quanta animi tranquillitate fruebar, quando in Domino gaudebam et exultabam in Deo Iesu meo. Ideo nunc magis doleo, quia scio quod perdidi; scio quam maxima bona amisi: ideo importune clamo: redde mihi laetitiam salutaris tui;

stone" [Luke 11:11-12]? If human fathers, even when they are
evil and sinners, want to give to their children the good things
you have given them, how much more will you, heavenly Father,
who are good by your essence, give the good Spirit to those who
ask you. See how your son, returned from a distant land, sorrowing and repentant, is asking you for the fish of faith. Just as a fish
lurks hidden underwater so is faith about things which are un-
seen. He asks, I say, for true faith so that he may rejoice in your
salvation. Are you going to hand him a serpent? Are you going to
give him the poisons of unbelief, which the tricky and ancient
serpent, the devil, puts forward? I beg from you, Lord, for the
egg of hope so that just as a chick is hoped for from the egg, so
may you grant me to go from hope to the vision of your salvation
so that out of that hope vision may come forth like a chick from
the egg. I beg for the egg of hope so that meanwhile my soul may
be uplifted by hope in this vale of tears and rejoice in your salvation. Are you going to give me the scorpion of despair so that,
just as the scorpion has its poison at the end of its tail, so I might
keep back a sin at the end of my life and entice myself with the
attractions of the world, just as from its face a scorpion seems
enticing? I also beg from you the bread of Christ's charity by
which he shares himself with everybody like bread so that I may
always rejoice in your salvation. Are you going to give me a stone,
that is, hardness of heart? Quite the contrary. Why then am I
hesitant to beg and request great things from you, Lord, since
you urge and invite me to beg and knock even to the point of
brashness?

What can I beg for which is more welcome to you and salu-
tary for me than that you give me the joy of your salvation? I have
already tasted how sweet the Lord is, how light and sweet is his
burden. I remember how I used to enjoy the peace, the tranquillity of soul when I rejoiced in the Lord and exulted in God, my
Jesus. Hence I am now in greater pain because I know what I
have lost, I know how I have missed out on the greatest goods.

redde quod propter peccata mea mihi abstulisti; redde quod mea
culpa perdidi: redde, obsecro, per merita eius qui semper stat ad
dexteram tuam et interpellat pro nobis, ut per ipsum sentiam te
mihi placatum, ut sit signaculum super cor meum, ut dicam cum
Apostolo: "Christo confixus sum cruci; vivo autem non ego; vivit
vero in me Christus." Verum quia magna est fragilitas mea, Spiritu
principali confirma me, ut nullis perturbationibus a Christo
separari valeam, nullis terroribus a te recedere, nullis cruciatibus
infirmari. Non enim virtus mea tanta est ut pugnare possit cum
antiquo serpente et ei praevalere. Petrus me docuit quanta sit
infirmitas nostra. Ipse vidit te, Domine Iesu, et tecum
familiarissime conversatus est; gloriam tuam in monte gustavit
quando transfiguratus es; vocem Patris audivit; mira opera tua
oculis suis conspexit; ipse quoque virtute tua miracula plura fecit;
super aquas pedibus ambulavit; verba tua tam potentia, tam suavia
quotidie audivit; ferventissimae fidei videbatur, dicebatque se
paratum tecum in carcerem et in mortem ire; et cum negationem
ipsius denuntiares ei, non tibi credebat; in virtute sua confidebat:
magis sibi homini quam tibi Deo fidem adhibebat. At cum ancilla
dixit ei: "Tu de illis es," illico territus negavit. Venit alia ancilla et
dixit: "Vere tu ex illis es." Iterum negavit. Non potuit coram
muliercula stare. Quomodo stetisset coram regibus et tyrannis?
Et cum iterum ab astantibus interrogaretur et accusaretur, coepit
iurare et detestari quia non novisset te. Quid, putas, dicebat?
Arbitror quod per Deum et per legem Moysi iurabat quod te non
noverat, et detestabatur dicens: "Putatis vos me discipulum esse
huius Samaritani seductoris et daemoniaci, qui nostram legem
destruxit? Ego discipulus sum Moysi: hunc autem nescio unde
sit." Deo gratias quia cessavit interrogatio! Si enim non cessasset

Hence I shout out stridently: "Give me back the joy of your salvation. Give back what you took away from me because of my
sins. Give back what I lost by my own fault. Give it back, I pray,
through the merits of him who always stands at your right hand
and intercedes for us so that I can feel that through him you are
pleased with me, that there be a sign over my heart, that I may
say with the Apostle, 'With Christ I am nailed to the cross; I live,
now not I, but Christ lives in me'" [Gal 2:20]. Because my weakness is great, strengthen me with a willing Spirit so that I cannot
be separated from Christ because of any troubles, nor fall away
from you because of any fears, nor be made weak by any tor-
ments. My strength is not great enough that it can fight against
the ancient serpent and prevail against him. Peter taught me how
weak we are. He saw you, Lord Jesus, and lived with you on a
very familiar basis; he tasted your glory on the mountain when
you were transfigured; he heard the voice of the Father; he saw
with his own eyes your marvelous works. By your power he worked
many miracles; he walked on foot over the waters; daily he heard
your words which were so powerful and sweet. He seemed to
have the most fervent faith and said he was ready to go with you
to jail and unto death; and when you brought against him his
own denial, he did not believe you. He trusted in his own strength:
he had more faith in himself a man than in you his God. But
when the servant girl said to him, "You belong to them," he was
instantly terrified and denied it. Another servant girl came and
said, "You are certainly one of them." Again he denied it. He
could not stand up to a young woman. How could he have stood
up to kings and despots? And when bystanders again questioned
and accused him, he began to swear and mouth oaths that he did
not know you. What, think you, was he saying? I calculate that
he swore an oath by God and by the law of Moses that he did not
know you and that he testified and said, "You think I am a disciple of that devil-possessed Samaritan trickster who has destroyed
our law? I am a disciple of Moses. I don't know where that fellow

interrogatio, nec quidem cessasset negatio: et si illae interrogationes
mille fuissent, negationes mille, immo mille periuria et
detestationes. Sed hae interrogationes fuerunt verba. Quid, ergo,
si Judaei venissent ad verbera? Nihil certe Petrus reliquisset quo
se, per negationes et periuria, detestationes et blasphemias, de
manibus eorum explicuisset. Tu autem, pie Domine, respexisti
eum, et statim peccatum suum cognovit. Nec tamen ausus est in
medium prosilire et confiteri te Filium Dei esse, quia nondum
confirmatus erat virtute ex alto. Nam procul dubio te iterum
negasset si flagella praeparata sibi vidisset: ideo maturiore consilio
egressus est foras, et flevit amare. Tu vero post resurrectionem
tuam apparuisti ei, consolatus es eum: nihilominus latebat propter
metum Judaeorum. Vidit te in caelum tam gloriose ascendentem,
et angelorum visione consolationeque confortatus est; nec tamen
in publicum adhinc prodire audebat. Experientia quippe didicerat
fragilitatem suam; probaverat infirmitatem; ideo expectabat
promissum Spiritum Sanctum. Venit et replevit gratia pectus eius:
tunc prodiit, tunc loqui coepit, tunc virtute magna testimonium
resurrectionis tuae reddidit, tunc principes sacerdotum et reges
non timuit, sed gloriabatur in tribulationibus, crucemque pro
summis delitiis amplexabatur. Itaque, Domine, in Spiritu
principali confirma me, ut iugiter maneam in laetitia salutaris
tui: alioquin contra tot bella persistere non possum; "caro
concupiscit adversus spiritum"; mundus undique me premit;
diabolus non dormit. Da mihi virtutem Spiritus tui, ut "cadant a
latere meo mille et decem millia a dextris meis," et sim fidelis et
fortis testis fidei tuae. Si enim Petrus, quem tot muneribus et
gratiis donaveras, ita miserabiliter cecidit, quid ego, Domine, quid
facerem, qui nec te in carne vidi, nec gloriam tuam in monte

is from." Thank God the questioning stopped. Had the questioning not stopped, the denials would surely not have stopped. Had there been a thousand of those questionings, there would have been a thousand denials, even a thousand lies and oaths. But these questionings were words. What then, if the Jews had come to scourgings? Certainly Peter would have stopped at nothing so that he could free himself from their hands by his denials and lies, his oaths and blasphemies. But you, O kind Lord, glanced at him, and he instantly recognized his sin. But he did not dare to jump into their midst and confess you as the Son of God, because he was not yet strengthened in virtue from on high. For he would undoubtedly have denied you again if he had seen whips being fetched for him. Therefore taking the wiser course he went outside and wept bitterly [Luke 22:54-62]. After your resurrection you appeared to him and consoled him; nevertheless he went into hiding for fear of the Jews. He saw you ascending in such glory into heaven and was strengthened by vision and consolation of angels, but he still did not dare as yet to come out in public. His experience had taught him his fragility, it showed his weakness, so he waited for the promised Holy Spirit. He came and filled his breast with grace. Then he went forth, then he began to speak, then he gave witness to your resurrection with great courage, then he did not fear the high priests and kings but gloried in his sufferings and embraced the cross as a supreme delight.

Lord, strengthen me then with a willing Spirit so that I may abide constantly in the joy of your salvation, otherwise I cannot stand up against so many wars. "The flesh lusts against the spirit" [Gal 5:17]. The world presses against me on all sides. The devil sleeps not. Give me the power of your Spirit so that "a thousand may fall at my side and ten thousand at my right hand" [Ps 91:7] and I be a faithful and strong witness to your faith. If Peter, on whom you heaped so many gifts and graces, fell so miserably, what would I do, what indeed, O Lord, who neither saw you in

gustavi, nec miracula tua conspexi, quinimmo opera tua mirifica
vix a longe intellexi, tuamque vocem numquam audivi, sed in
peccatis semper fui? Spiritu itaque principali confirma me, ut in
tuo obsequio perseverare valeam et dare pro te animam meam.

"Docebo iniquos vias tuas et impii ad te convertentur."
Non hoc, Domine, temeritati ascribas si docere cupio iniquos
vias tuas. Non enim iniquus, infamis et in vinculis, iniquos docere
cupio, sed si reddideris mihi laetitiam salutaris tui. Si me Spiritu
principali confirmaveris, si me liberum miseris, tunc docebo
iniquos vias tuas. Non enim est hoc tibi difficile, qui de lapidibus
potes suscitare filios Habrahae. Nec peccata possunt obstare tibi
si volueris hoc facere: quinimmo "ubi abundavit peccatum,
superabundavit et gratia." Paulus spirans minarum et caedis in
discipulos Domini potestatem accepit, ut si quos inveniret viros
ac mulieres te sequentes tuamque fidem confitentes, vinctos
perduceret in Hierusalem. Ibat igitur furiis invectus, sicut lupus
rapax, ut oves tuas disperderet, raperet et occideret. Dum ergo
esset in via, in fervore persecutionis, in actu peccati, dum te
persequeretur, dum tuos occidere vellet, dum nulla ei inesset ad
gratiam praeparatio nullaque peccati cognitio, quando totis viribus
tibi adversabatur, te blasphemabat, teque detestabatur, ecce vox
pietatis tuae super eum, dicens: "Saule, Saule, quid me
persequeris?" Qua voce illico prostratus et erectus est: prostratus
corpore, erectus mente. Excitasti dormientem, aperuisti oculos
somno gravatos, infudisti iucem tuam, ostendisti faciem tuam,
effudisti ineffabilem misericordiam tuam. Surrexit mortuus,
oculos aperuit, vidit te et ait: "Domine, quid me vis facere?" Misisti
lupum ad agnum; misisti eum ad Ananiam. Baptizatus est et

the flesh nor tasted your glory on the mountain, nor witnessed your miracles? Even more, I have barely understood your marvels at a distance and have never heard your voice, but have always lived in sin. Strengthen me then with a willing Spirit so that I may be able to persevere in your service and give my soul for you.

"I will teach transgressors your paths, and the wicked will be converted to you" [Ps 51:13].

Do not attribute it to my rashness, O Lord, if I desire to teach transgressors your paths. It is not I, the transgressor in disrepute and in chains, who desires to teach transgressors, but I to whom you have given back the joy of your salvation. If you strengthen me with a willing Spirit, if you set me free, then will I teach transgressors your ways. This is not something difficult for you, who can raise up children of Abraham from stones. Neither can my sins stand in your way if you want to do this; indeed, "where sin abounds, grace also abounds even more" [Rom 5:20].

Paul, breathing out threats and slaughter against the Lord's disciples, received the power to lead back to Jerusalem in chains any men and women he found who were following you and confessing your faith. He went about driven by frenzy like a ravening wolf to scatter, seize and kill your sheep. While he was on the road ardent to persecute, in the act of sin, while he was persecuting you, while he desired to kill your people, while there was in him no preparation for grace and no knowledge of his sin, when he was working against you with all his might, blaspheming you, hating you—look, the voice of your kindness was upon him and said: "Saul, Saul, why are you persecuting me" [Acts 9:4]? By that voice he was immediately knocked flat and stood upright: knocked flat in body, stood upright in mind. You awakened the sleeper, you opened eyes heavy with sleep, you poured in your light, you showed your face, you poured forth your indescribable mercy. The dead man arose, opened his eyes, saw you and said, "Lord, what do you want me to do" [Acts 9:6]? You sent a wolf to a

repente, Spiritu Sancto repletus, factus est vas electionis ad portandum nomen tuum coram gentibus et regibus et filiis Israel. Continuo, ergo, ingressus synagogas, intrepidus praedicavit te, affirmans quoniam tu es Christus. Disputabat, invalescebat et confundebat Judaeos. Ecce, Domine, quia statim de persecutore fecisti praedicatorem et talem ac tam magnum ut plus caeteris apostolis laboraverit. O mira virtus tua! Si volueris de iniquo facere iustum, de persecutore praedicatorem, quis prohibebit? Quis resistet tibi? Quis dicere poterit: "Cur ita facis?" Omnia quaecumque voluisti, fecisti in caelo et in terra, in mari et in omnibus abyssis. Non ergo arrogantiae imputetur, si non mea sed tua virtute docere cupio iniquos vias tuas. Scio enim me nihil tibi offerte posse quod oculis tuae pietatis magis placeat: hoc sacrificium est omnium maximum. Nihil etiam possum facere mihi utilius. Si ergo me in alium virum mutaveris, docebo iniquos vias tuas: non vias Platonis, non Aristotelis, non implicationes syllogismorum, non philosophiae dogmata, non rhetorum inflammata verba, non negotia saecularia, non vias vanitatis, non vias ducentes ad mortem; sed vias tuas et praecepta tua, quae ducunt ad vitam, non unam viam tantum, sed multas vias, quia multa sunt praecepta tua. Omnes tamen istae viae terminantur ad unam; omnes enim in una copulantur caritate, quae adeo coniungit animos fidelium, ut fiat in eis "cor unum et anima una" in Domino. Vel certe diversae viae, diversae sunt vitae: per aliam namque incedunt clerici, per aliam monachi, per aliam mendicantes; aliam tenent matrimonio coniuncti, aliam in viduitate degentes et continentes, aliam virgines; aliam sequuntur principes, aliam doctores, aliam mercatores: denique diversi status hominum per diversas vias ad patriam caelestem proficiscuntur. Docebo itaque iniquos vias tuas unumquemque iuxta condi-

lamb, you sent him to Ananias. He was baptized, and suddenly he was filled with the Holy Spirit and made a vessel of election to carry your name before nations and kings and the children of Israel. So immediately he entered the synagogue and preached you fearlessly, asserting that you are the Christ. He engaged in debates, grew stronger and refuted the Jews. See, Lord, how you instantly made a persecutor into a preacher, and such a gifted and great one that he outworked the other apostles [Acts 9:1-22].

Marvelous is your strength! Who will stop you, if you should want to make a just person out of a transgressor, a preacher out of a persecutor? Who can resist you? Who could say to you, "Why are you acting this way?" All whatsoever you wanted, you did in heaven and on earth, in the sea and in all its depths. Let it not be put down to rashness if I desire to teach transgressors your paths— not by my power, but yours. For I know that I can offer you nothing which is more pleasing to your kindly eyes: this is the greatest sacrifice of all. There is also nothing I can do which is more useful for me. If then you change me into another man, I will teach transgressors your paths: not the paths of Plato nor Aristotle, not the intricacies of syllogisms, the dogmas of philosophy, not the fiery words of the rhetoricians, not worldly business, not the paths of vanity, not paths that lead to death, but your paths and your commandments which lead to life, not one path only but many paths because you have many commandments. But all these paths end up in one, for all are joined together in a single charity which so joins together the souls of believers that there comes to exist in them "one heart and one soul" [Acts 4:32] in the Lord. There are certainly different paths and different lives: clerics go by one path, monks by another, friars by another; people joined in marriage take a different path, those living chastely in widowhood take another, virgins another. Princes follow another path, teachers another, merchants another. Finally the various classes of people make progress toward their heavenly fatherland by different paths. I shall then teach trans-

tionem et captum suum; et impii ad te convertentur, quia
praedicabo eis non me ipsum sed Christum crucifixum. Ideo non
ad laudes meas sed ad te convertentur. Relinquent enim vias suas,
ut venientes ad tuas, per eas incedant et ad te perveniant.

"Libera me de sanguinibus, Deus, Deus salutis meae, et
exultabit lingua mea iustitiam tuam."

In multis sanguinibus suffocor et de profundis eorum clamo
ad te: "Domine, Domine, exaudi vocem meam." Ne differas,
Domine, quia morti proximus sum: sanguines mei peccata mea
sunt. Sicut enim in sanguine est vita carnis, ita in peccato est vita
peccatoris. Effunde sanguinem, moritur animal: effunde per
confessionem peccatum, moritur peccator et iustus efficitur. Ego
igitur non solum in sanguine involutus sum, sed etiam in
sanguinibus immersus: gurgites sanguinum me trahunt ad inferos.
Succurre mihi, Domine, ne peream. Libera me de sanguinibus,
Deus, qui omnia gubernas et moves, qui solus potes me liberare,
in cuius manu est omnis spiritus vitae. Libera me de sanguinibus,
Deus, auctor salutis meae; Deus, in quo solo est salus mea. Libera
me, Domine, sicut liberasti Noe de aquis diluvii. Libera me sicut
liberasti Loth de incendio Sodomorum. Libera me sicut liberasti
filios Israel de profundo Maris Rubri. Libera me sicut liberasti
Ionam de ventre ceti. Libera me sicut liberasti tres pueros de
camino ignis ardentis. Libera me sicut liberasti Petrum de periculo
maris. Libera me sicut liberasti Paulum de profundo pelagi. Libera
me sicut liberasti infinitos peccatores de manu mortis et de portis
inferni; et exultabit lingua mea iustitiam tuam, idest propter
iustitiam tuam, quam in me sentiam per gratiam tuam. "Iustitia
enim tua," ut dicit Apostolus, "est per fidem Iesu Christi in omnes
et super omnes qui credunt in eum." Exultabit itaque lingua mea

gressors your paths according to the condition and capacity of each individual. The wicked will be converted to you because I will preach to them not myself but Christ crucified. Therefore they will be converted to you, not to my praises. They will leave their own paths in order to come to yours; let them walk along them and come to you.

"Deliver me from bloodguilt, God, God of my salvation, and my tongue shall sing of your justice" [Ps 51:14].

I am suffocating in my great bloodguilt and from its depth I call out to you, "Lord, Lord, hear my voice" [Ps 130:1]. Don't delay, Lord, because I am near death. My sins are my bloodguilt. Just as the life of flesh lies in its blood, so the life of the sinner is in sin. Pour out its blood and the animal dies. Pour out your sin through confession, and the sinner dies and is made just. Therefore I am not only involved in blood, but I am also immersed in bloodguilt. Torrents of bloodguilt are carrying me off to hell. Help me, Lord, lest I perish. Free me from bloodguilt, O God, who controls and moves all things, who alone can free me, in whose hand is every breath of life. Free me from bloodguilt, God, author of my salvation, God in whom alone is my salvation. Free me, Lord, as you freed Noah from the waters of the flood. Free me as you freed Lot from the conflagration of the Sodomites. Free me as you freed the children of Israel from the depth of the Red Sea. Free me as you freed Jonah from the belly of the whale. Free me as you freed the three young men in the furnace of burning fire. Free me as you freed Peter from the danger of the sea. Free me as you freed Paul from the depths of the open sea. Free me as you freed countless sinners from the hand of death and the gates of hell. My tongue shall sing of your justice, that is, because of your justice that I experience in myself because of your grace. As the Apostle said, "Your justice is through the faith in Jesus Christ for all and upon all who believe in him" [Rom 3:22]. So

laudando hanc iustitiam tuam, extollendo gratiam tuam, magnificando pietatem tuam, confitendo peccata mea, ut in me laudetur misericordia tua, quae tam magnum peccatorem dignata sit iustificare, ut cognoscant omnes homines quod salvas sperantes in te, et liberas eos de manu angustiae, Domine Deus noster.

"Domine, labia mea aperies, et os meum annuntiabit laudem tuam."

Magna res est laus tua, Domine, et de tuo fonte procedit, de quo non bibit peccator. "Non est enim speciosa laus in ore peccatoris." Libera ergo me de sanguinibus, Deus, Deus salutis meae, et exultabit lingua mea iustitiam tuam. Tunc, Domine, labia mea aperies, et os meum annuntiabit laudem tuam. Tu enim habes clavem David: "qui claudis et nemo aperit, et aperis et nemo claudit." Tunc ergo aperies labia mea, sicut aperuisti labia "infantium et lactentium, ex quorum ore perfecisti laudem tuam." Hi profecto fuerunt prophetae et apostoli, caeteri quoque sancti tui, qui te simplici et puro corde et ore laudabant, non autem philosophi et oratores, qui dixerunt: "Linguam nostram magnificabimus, et labia nostra a nobis sunt. Quis noster Deus est?" Aperiebant ipsi labia sua; non tu aperiebas ea: ideo ex eorum ore non perfecisti laudem. Infantes tui, Domine, laudabant te, et se ipsos despiciebant. Philosophi, dum te laudare gestiebant, se ipsos magnificare volebant. Lactentes tui laudabant gloriam tuam, quam per gratiam supercaelestem cognoscebant. Philosophi, per sola naturalia te cognoscentes, laudes tuas perfecte exprimere non poterant. Sancti tui te corde et ore et bonis operibus laudabant: philosophi solum verbis et inflata sapientia. Pueri tui in toto terrarum orbe laudes tuas diffuderunt: philosophi vix paucis

my tongue shall sing by praising this justice of yours, by extolling your grace, by glorifying your kindness, by confessing my sins so that your mercy may be praised in me. Your mercy has deigned to justify such a great sinner so that all people may realize that you save those who hope in you and free them from the hand of trouble, O Lord, our God.

"Lord, open my lips, and my mouth will proclaim your praise" [Ps 51:15].

Your praise is a great thing, O Lord, and comes forth from your fountain, of which the sinner drinks not. "Praise is not beautiful in the mouth of a sinner" [Sir 15:9]. Free me then from bloodguilt, God, God of my salvation, and my tongue shall sing of your justice. Then, O Lord, will you open my lips and my mouth shall proclaim your praise. "The key of David is held" by you, "who shut and no one opens, who open and no one shuts" [Rev 3:7]. Then will you open my lips just as you opened the lips "of infants and babies at the breast and from them you perfected your praise" [Ps 8:2].

The prophets and apostles, along with your other saints, were those who praised you with a simple and pure heart and mouth, but not the philosophers and orators who said, "We shall glorify our own tongue, and our lips are with us. Who is our God" [Ps 12:4]? They themselves opened their lips; you did not open them; therefore you have not perfected the praise from their mouth. Your infants have been praising you, O Lord, and they did not esteem themselves. The philosophers, while they made a show of praising you, wanted to glorify themselves. But your babies at the breast praised your glory, which they knew through your supercelestial grace. The philosophers, who knew you through natural phenomena alone, could not perfectly express your praises. Your saints praised you with their hearts and their mouths and their good works, the philosophers did so only with words and puffed-up wisdom. Your children spread your praises through

discipulis praedicaverunt. Amici tui laudibus tuis innumerabiles homines a peccatis ad virtutes et ad veram felicitatem convertebant: philosophi nec veras virtutes nec veram felicitatem cognoscebant. Dilecti tui ineffabilem pietatem tuam, quam ostendisti in Filio caritatis tuae, praedicaverunt: philosophi hanc nullo pacto intelligere potuerunt. Ex ore itaque infantium et lactentium perfecisti laudem tuam. Semper enim tibi placuit exaltare humiles et humiliare superbos. Quia ergo superbis semper resistis, da mihi veram humilitatem, ut ex ore meo perficias laudem tuam. Da mihi cor parvuli, quia, nisi conversus fuero sicut parvulus, non potero introire in regnum caelorum. Fac me sicut unum de infantibus et lactentibus tuis, ut semper pendeam ab uberibus sapientiae tuae, quia "meliora sunt ubera eius vino," et "melior est sapientia cunctis opibus, et omnia quae desiderantur huic non valent comparari." "Infinitus enim thesaurus est hominibus, quo qui usi sunt participes facti sunt amicitiae Dei." Si ergo me parvulum feceris, laudem tuam in ore meo perficies. Tunc enim aperies labia mea, et os meum annuntiabit laudem tuam. Annuntiabit quippe perfecte, sicut ex ore infantium et lactentium perfecisti laudem.

"Quoniam si voluisses sacrificium, dedissem utique; holocaustis non delectaberis."

Os meum, Domine, annuntiabit laudem tuam. Scio enim hoc tibi gratissimum esse, cum per Prophetam dicas: "Sacrificium laudis honorificabit me; et illic iter quo ostendam illi salutare Dei." Offeram itaque laudem tibi, laudem, inquam, infantium et lactentium pro omnibus peccatis meis. Et quare laudem potius quam sacrificium offeram tibi pro omnibus peccatis meis? quoniam, si voluisses sacrificium, dedissem utique; holocaustis non delectaberis. Numquid sanguine hircorum aut vitulorum

the whole earth; the philosophers preached to barely a handful of disciples. By praising you your friends were converting countless people from their sins to virtues and true happiness; the philosophers recognized neither true virtues nor true happiness. Your loved ones preached the indescribable kindness which you showed in the Son of your love; the philosophers were totally incapable of knowing this. Therefore you have perfected your praise from the mouth of infants and babies at the breast.

It always pleased you to exalt the humble and cast down the proud. Since then you always resist the proud, grant me true humility so that from my mouth you may perfect your praise. Grant me the heart of a child, because unless I am converted and become like a child, I will not be able to enter into the kingdom of heaven. Make me like one of your infants and babies at the breast, so that I may always lay at the breasts of your wisdom, because "her breasts are better than wine" [Cant 1:2] and "better is wisdom than all riches, and all things which are desired cannot be compared to it" [Prov 8:11]. "It is an infinite treasure for those who by using it are made partakers in God's friendship" [Wis 7:14]. If then you make me a child, you will perfect your praise in my mouth. For then you will open my lips, and my mouth will proclaim your praise. Indeed, it will proclaim it perfectly, just as you have perfected praise from the mouths of infants and babies at the breast.

"For if you had desired sacrifice, I would have gladly given it, but you will not delight in holocausts" [Ps 51:16].

My mouth, O Lord, will proclaim your praise. I know that this is most welcome to you since you say through the prophet, "A sacrifice of praise will honor me, and I will show the person who walks honestly the salvation of God" [Ps 50:23]. I shall then offer praise to you, the praise, I say, of infants and babies at the breast, for all my sins. Why shall I offer you praise rather than sacrifice for all my sins? Because had you wished a sacrifice, I

placari poteris? Numquid manducabis carnem taurorum, aut
sanguinem hircorum potabis? An forte aurum quaeris, qui caelum
et terram possides? Num vis ut corpus meum sacrificem tibi, qui
non vis mortem peccatoris, sed magis "ut convertatur et vivat"?
Castigabo tamen cum mensura carnem meam, ut per gratiam
tuam rationi subiecta sit eique deserviat: nam et in hoc si
mensuram excessero, mihi imputabis ad peccatum. "Rationabile,"
inquit Apostolus tuus, "obsequium vestrum." Tu quoque dixisti
per Prophetam: "Misericordiam volo et non sacrificium." Igitur
os meum annuntiabit laudem tuam, quia haec oblatio honorificat
te, et ostendit nobis iter ad salutare tuum. "Paratum cor meum,
Deus; paratum cor meum"; paratum per gratiam tuam ad omnia
quae tibi grata sunt facienda. Hoc unum inveni tibi acceptissi-
mum; hoc offeram tibi; hoc semper erit in corde meo; hoc
personabunt labia mea: quoniam si voluisses sacrificium corporale,
utique dedissem. Paratum enim cor meum per gratiam tuam, ut
impleat voluntatem tuam: sed huiusmodi holocaustis non
delectaberis. Corpora enim fecisti propter spiritum: ideo tu
spiritualia et non corporea quaeris. Dicis enim in quodam loco:
"Praebe, Fili mi, cor tuum mihi," hoc est sacrificium quod tibi
placet. Cor, dolore peccatorum et amore caelestium bonorum
inflammatum, offeratur tibi, et nequaquam amplius repetatur:
huiusmodi holocausto tu delectaberis.

"Sacrificium Deo spiritus contribulatus: cor contritum et
humiliatum, Deus, non despicies."

Spiritus quidem contribulatus, non caro contribulata tibi
placet. Nam caro contribulatur quia terrena quae optat, non habet,
vel certe in se sentit quae odit. Spiritus vero contribulatur de culpa,
eo quod sit contra Deum quem amat. Dolet se suum creatorem

would certainly have given it, but you will not delight in holocausts. Are you likely to be pleased by the blood of goats or calves? Are you going to eat the flesh of bulls or drink the blood of goats? Or maybe you are looking for gold—you who possess heaven and earth? Do you want me to sacrifice my body to you—you who do not wish the death of the sinner but rather that "he be converted and live" [Ezek 18:23]? Shall I nonetheless chastise my flesh with moderation so that through grace it be subjected to reason and subservient to it? For if in this I shall exceed moderation, you will count it against me as a sin. Your Apostle says, "Your worship should be reasonable" [Rom 12:1]. You also said through the Prophet, "I want mercy and not sacrifice" [Hos 6:6]. Therefore my mouth shall proclaim your praise, because this offering honors you and shows us the road to your salvation. "My heart is ready, God, my heart is ready" [Ps 108:1]; ready by your grace to do all things which are pleasing to you. This one thing I have found is most acceptable to you; this I offer you; this will always be in my heart; this will sound on my lips: had you wanted a bodily sacrifice, I would have certainly given it. My heart is ready through your grace to fulfill your will: but in that sort of sacrifice you take no delight. You made the body for the spirit, so you are looking for things spiritual and not corporeal. In a certain place you say, "Offer me, my child, your heart" [Prov 23:26]. That is a sacrifice which pleases you. The heart inflamed with sorrow over its sins and with love of heavenly goods may be offered to you, and nothing more at all will be asked for: this is the sort of holocaust you will delight in.

"A sacrifice to God is a broken spirit, a heart contrite and humbled, O God, you will not despise" [Ps 51: 17].

A broken spirit, not broken flesh, truly pleases you. The flesh is broken because it does not have the earthly things it desires or surely feels within itself what it hates. But the spirit is broken over guilt because it is against the God whom it loves. It is sor-

et redemptorem offendisse, se sanguinem eius despexisse, se tam bonum et dulcem patrem contempsisse. Hic ergo spiritus contribulatus sacrificium est tibi odoris suavissimi: ex aromatibus enim amarissimis, idest ex memoria peccatorum, conficitur. Dum enim peccata in mortariolo cordis colliguntur et pistillo contritionis contunduntur, in pulveremque rediguntur atque aquis lacrimarum humectantur, inde fit unguentum et sacrificium suavissimum tibi, quod oblatum nequaquam despicies. Nam cor contritum et humiliatum, Deus, non despicies. Qui ergo cor suum saxeum, ex durissimis peccatorum lapidibus constructum, frangit et conterit, ut inde unguentum conficiat contritionis in abundantia lacrimarum, et de peccatorum gravitate aut multitudine minime desperans, humiliter tibi huiusmodi sacrificium offert, nullo modo a te despicitur: quia cor contritum et humiliatum, Deus, non despicies. Maria Magdalena, in civitate peccatrix, tale unguentum confecit; in alabastro cordis posuit; domum pharisaei ingredi non timuit; secus pedes tuos prostrata est; flere inter epulas non erubuit, dolore pressa non loquebatur, sed cor eius in lacrimis solvebatur, quibus lavit pedes tuos, capillis suis tersit, unguento unxit, et osculari non cessavit. Quis audivit unquam tale, aut quis vidit huic simile? Placuit itaque tibi hoc eius sacrificium, et adeo gratum fuit ut pharisaeo, qui iustus videbatur, eam praetuleris. Verbis enim tuis insinuasti tantum distare inter iustificationem Mariae et iustitiam pharisaei quantum inter se distant lavare pedes aqua et abluere lacrimis, osculari semel faciem et non cessare osculari pedes, ungere caput oleo et ungere pedes unguento pretiosissimo. Quin immo longe amplius Maria praestabat pharisaeo, quia ipse nec aquam, nec osculum, nec oleum tibi exhibuerat. O magna virtus tua, Domine! magna

rowful for having offended its creator and redeemer, for having despised his blood, for having held such a good and sweet Father in contempt. This broken spirit is therefore the most sweet sacrifice to you: it is made up from bitter perfumes, that is, from the memory of its sins. While your sins are collected in the mortar basin of your heart and crushed with the pestle of contrition, they are ground into dust and moistened with the water of tears; from them comes an ointment and sacrifice most sweet to you, which you will in no way despise when it is offered. O God, you do not despise a broken and contrite heart. Therefore you will in no way spurn the person who breaks and crushes a stony heart, which is put together from the hardest rocks of sins, and makes from it an ointment of contrition with an abundance of tears and does not in the least despair over the seriousness or number of one's sins and humbly offers you this kind of sacrifice. For you will not despise a contrite and humbled heart.

Mary Magdalene, the town prostitute, made such an ointment. She put it in the alabaster jar of her heart; she did not fear to enter the home of the Pharisee; she prostrated herself at your feet; she was not ashamed to weep in the midst of a banquet. Weighed down with sorrow she did not speak but did open her heart in the tears with which she washed your feet; she dried them with her hair, anointed them with ointment and did not cease to kiss them. Who ever heard of such a thing, or who has seen its like? Her sacrifice pleased you, and was so welcome to you that you rated her above the Pharisee, who seemed just. You insinuated by your words that there was as much difference between the justification of Mary and the justice of the Pharisee as there is difference between washing feet with water and bathing them in tears, between giving a single kiss on the face and kissing the feet unceasingly, between anointing the head with oil and anointing the feet with very precious ointment. Indeed, Mary far surpassed the Pharisee because he offered you neither water nor a kiss nor oil [Luke 7:36-46].

potentia tua, quae se, maxime parcendo et miserando, manifestat! Video, igitur, quia cor contritum et humiliatum, Deus, non despicis! Idcirco huiusmodi cor tibi offerre studeo, nec oportet me hoc verbis suadere, quia tu es "Deus qui scrutaris renes et corda." Suscipe ergo et hoc sacrificium meum, quod si forte imperfectum est, tu, qui solus potes, ipsum perfice, ut fiat holocaustum, idest totum incensum ardore tuae immensae caritatis, ut tibi placeat, aut ut saltem ipsum non despicias. Si enim non despexeris, scio quod inveniam gratiam coram te, et posthac nullus sanctorum tuorum, sive in caelo sive in terra, me despiciet.

"Benigne fac, Domine, in bona voluntate tua Syon, ut aedificentur muri Hierusalem."

Quia enim scriptum est: "Cum sancto sanctus eris, et cum viro innocente innocens eris, et cum electo electus eris, et cum perverso perverteris," valde cupio omnes homines "salvos fieri et ad agnitionem tui nominis venire." Hoc enim est eis necessarium, et mihi utile esset, nam eorum orationibus, meritis et exemplis resurgerem, et ad meliora quotidie provocarer. Rogo ergo te, Domine, quamvis peccator: benigne fac in bona voluntate tua Syon, ut aedificentur muri Hierusalem. Syon est Ecclesia tua, nam Syon interpretatur "specula," quia Ecclesia tua, per gratiam Spiritus Sancti, gloriam Dei pro captu huius vitae speculatur. Hinc dicebat Apostolus: "Nos revelata facie gloriam Domini speculantes in eandem imaginem transformamur a claritate in claritatem tamquam a Domini Spiritu." Domine Deus, quam parva est hodie Ecclesia tua! Nam totus mundus deficit, nam longe plures sunt infideles quam christiani. Inter christianos autem ubi sunt qui, relictis terrenis, gloriam Domini speculentur? Paucos certe,

Great is your strength, O Lord, great is your power, which manifests itself above all in sparing and being compassionate! I see then, O God, how you do not despise a contrite and humbled heart. Hence I am eager to offer you that sort of heart, and I do not have to make a case for this with words, because you are "a God who searches the reins and hearts" [Ps 7:9]. Accept then this sacrifice of mine; if it is perhaps imperfect, make it perfect yourself, as you alone can, in order that it becomes a holocaust, that is, something totally consumed by the heat of your boundless charity, so that it be pleasing to you or at least not despised by you. If you do not despise it, I know I will find favor before you and henceforward none of your saints, whether in heaven or on earth, will despise me.

"Treat your Zion with kindness in your good will, Lord, so that the walls of Jerusalem may be built up" [Ps 51:18].

For it is written: "With the holy you will be holy, and with the innocent you will be innocent, and with the elect you will be elect, and with the perverse you will deal perversely" [Ps 18:25-26]; I strongly desire all people "to be saved and come to the knowledge of your name" [1 Tim 2:4]. This is needful for them and helpful for me, for I rise up through their prayers, merits, and examples and am daily stimulated to better things. I therefore beg you, O Lord, even though I am a sinner: treat your Zion with kindness in your good will so that the walls of Jerusalem may be built up. Zion is your Church, for Zion is interpreted "watchtower," because your Church through the grace of the Holy Spirit stands watch for the glory of God as far as this is possible in this life. Hence the Apostle said, "We with unveiled face beholding the glory of God are transformed into that same image, from brightness into brightness, as by the Spirit of the Lord" [2 Cor 3:18]. Lord God, how small is your Church today! For the whole world falls away, for there are far more unbelievers than Christians. Among Christians, however, where are those who watch

invenies, comparatione eorum "qui terrena sapiunt, quorum deus venter est, et gloria in confusione ipsorum." Benigne fac in bona voluntate tua Syon, ut augeatur merito et numero. Respice de caelo, et fac benigne iuxta consuetudinem tuam, ut ignem caritatis de caelo emittas super nos, qui consumat omnia peccata nostra. Fac, Domine, benigne in bona voluntate tua, "ut non secundum peccata nostra facias nobis, neque secundum iniquitates nostras retribuas nobis," sed fac nobis secundum magnam misericordiam tuam. Tu, Domine, Pater noster et Redemptor noster, tu pax et gaudium nostrum, tu spes nostra et salus aeterna: "omnes a te bona expectant. Dante te illis colligent; aperiente te manum tuam, omnia implebuntur bonitate; avertente autem te faciem, turbabuntur. Auferes spiritum eorum et deficient, et in pulverem suum revertentur. Emitte spiritum tuum et creabuntur, et renovabis faciem terrae." Domine, obsecro, quae utilitas in damnatione tot millium hominum? Infernus impletur; Ecclesia quotidie evacuatur. "Exurge! Quare obdormis, Domine? Exurge, et ne repellas in finem." Benigne fac in bona voluntate tua Syon, ut aedificentur muri Hierusalem. Quid est Hierusalem, quae interpretatur "visio pacis," nisi beatorum civitas sancta, quae est mater nostra? Huius muri corruerunt quando Lucifer cum angelis suis corruit: in quorum loca assumuntur homines iusti. Denigne fac igitur, Domine, Syon, ut cito impleatur numerus electorum et aedificentur perficianturque muri Hierusalem ex lapidibus vivis, te semper laudantibus et permanentibus in aeternum.

out for the Lord's glory, having left behind worldly things? You will find them few indeed compared to those "whose minds are set on earthly things, whose god is their belly, and whose glory is in their shame" [Phil 3:19]. Treat Zion with kindness in your good will so that it may grow in merit and number. Look down from heaven and treat us with kindness, as you usually do, so that you send down from heaven the fire of charity upon us to burn up all our sins. Treat us with kindness, O Lord, in your good will "so that you deal with us not according to our sins nor repay us according to our iniquities" [Ps 103:10], but treat us according to your great mercy. You, O Lord, are our Father and our Redeemer, you are our peace and joy, you are our hope and eternal salvation: "All look to you for good things. You give, and they gather them up. You open your hand, and all things are filled with goodness, but if you turn away your face, they are dismayed. If you take away their breath, they grow weak and they are returned to their dust. Send forth your Spirit, and they will be created, and you will renew the face of the earth" [Ps 104:27-30].

I beg you, Lord, what advantage is there in the damnation of so many thousands of people? Hell is filled, the Church is daily emptied. "Arise! Why do you sleep, O Lord. Arise, and do not cast us off forever" [Ps 44:23]. Treat your Zion with kindness in your good will so that the walls of Jerusalem may be built up. What is Jerusalem, (the name means "vision of peace") if it is not the holy city of the blessed, which is our mother? Its walls fell down when Lucifer fell down with his angels. Just persons are assigned to take their places. Deal kindly then with Zion, O Lord, in order that the number of the elect may be quickly filled up and that the walls of Jerusalem may be built and completed with living stones who praise you always and remain in place unto eternity.

"Tunc acceptabis sacrificium iustitiae, oblationes et
holocausta; tunc imponent super altare tuum vitulos."

Tunc, cum benigne feceris in bona voluntate tua Syon,
acceptabis sacrificium iustitiae. Acceptabis, dico, quia igne tuae
caritatis consumes. Sic enim sacrificium Moysi et sacrificium
Heliae acceptasti. Tunc enim sacrificia iustitiae acceptas, quando
animas, quae iuste vivere satagunt, gratia tua impinguas. Quid
prodest sacrificia tibi offerre, quando non acceptas ea? O Domine,
quot offerimus hodie sacrificia, quae tibi grata non sunt, sed potius
abominabilia! Offerimus enim sacrificia non iustitiae, sed
caerimoniae nostrae: ideo non sunt tibi accepta. Ubi nunc
apostolorum gloria? ubi martyrum fortitudo? ubi praedicatorum
fructus? ubi monachorum sancta simplicitas? ubi primorum
christianorum virtutes et opera? Tunc enim acceptabas eorum
sacrificia, quando gratia tua et virtutibus eos exornabas. Si quoque
tu benigne feceris Syon in bona voluntate tua, tunc acceptabis
sacrificium iustitiae, quia populus incipiet bene vivere, et mandata
tua servare, ac iustitiam facere, et super ipsum erit benedictio
tua. Tunc oblationes sacerdotum et clericorum tibi acceptae erunt,
quia, relictis terrenis, ad perfectiorem vitam sese accingent, et
unctio benedictionis tuae erit super capita eorum. Tunc grata erunt
tibi holocausta religiosorum, qui, relicto torpore et tepiditate
eliminata, incendio divini amoris omni ex parte consumentur.
Tunc episcopi et praedicatores imponent super altare tuum vitulos,
quia, in omni virtute consumati et Spiritu Sancto repleti, non
dubitabunt ponere animas suas pro ovibus suis. Altare enim tuum
quid est nisi crux tua, bone Iesu, super quam oblatus fuisti? Quid
vitulus lasciviens significat nisi corpus nostrum? Tunc ergo
imponent super altare tuum vitulos, quando corpora sua offerent

"Then will you receive a sacrifice of justice, oblations and holocausts, then will they put calves upon your altar" [Ps 51:19].

Then, when you have treated your Zion with kindness in your good will, you will accept the sacrifice of justice. You will receive it, I say, because you will burn it up in the fire of your charity. Thus did you accept the sacrifice of Moses and the sacrifice of Elijah. Then may you accept sacrifices of justice when you fatten up with your grace the souls which strive to live justly. What good does it do to offer you sacrifices when you do not accept them. O Lord, how many sacrifices do we offer up today which are not pleasing to you but rather abominations! For we offer not sacrifices of justice but our ceremonies: that is why they are not acceptable to you. Where now is the glory of the apostles? Where the courage of the martyrs? Where the fruit of the preachers? Where the holy simplicity of the monks? Where the virtues and works of the first Christians? Back then you accepted their sacrifices when you endowed them with your grace and virtues. If you also were to treat Zion with kindness in your good will, then you will accept the sacrifice of justice because the people will begin to live in the right way, to keep your commandments, and to do justice, and upon them will be your blessing. Then will the oblations of the priests and clerics be acceptable to you because they have left behind earthly things and girded themselves for a more perfect life, and the anointing of your blessing will be upon their heads. Then will the holocausts of the members of religious orders be pleasing to you, for after putting aside tepidity and getting rid of their lukewarmness, they will be consumed by the fire of divine love in all their members. Then will bishops and preachers lay calves upon your altar because, after having been perfected in every virtue and filled with the Holy Spirit, they will not hesitate to lay down their lives for their sheep. What is your altar, if not your cross, good Jesus, upon which you were offered up? What does the lusty calf signify unless our body? Then will they lay upon your altar the calves when they offer up their bod-

cruci, idest cruciatibus et morti pro nomine tuo. Tunc florebit
Ecclesia; tunc dilatabit terminos suos; tunc laus tua resonabit ab
extremis terrae; tunc gaudium et laetitia occupabit orbem
terrarum; tunc "exultabunt sancti in gloria et laetabuntur in
cubilibus suis," expectantes nos in terra viventium. Fiat, obsecro,
Domine, nunc mihi illud "tunc," ut miserearis mei secundum
magnam misericordiam tuam, et suscipias me in sacrificium
iustitiae, in oblationem sanctimoniae, in holocaustum religiosae
vitae, et in vitulum crucis tuae, per quam transire merear ab hac
valle miseriae ad gloriam illam, "quam praeparasti diligentibus
te." Amen.

ies to the cross, that is, to tortures and death for your name. Then will the Church flourish; then will it expand its borders; then will your praise resound to the ends of the earth; then will joy and happiness take over the whole earth; then "will the saints exult in glory and rejoice on their couches" [Ps 149:5] as they await us in the land of the living. I beg you, Lord, that that "then" may become my "now" so that you take pity on me according to your great mercy, and that you receive me as a sacrifice of justice, as an oblation of holiness, as a holocaust of the religious life and as a calf of your cross; through the cross may I merit to pass over from this valley of misery to that glory "which you have prepared for those who love you" [1 Cor 2:9]. Amen.

Expositio in Psalmum "In te, Domine, speravi"

Exposition of the Psalm "In You, O Lord, Have I Hoped"

Expositio in Psalmum
"In te, Domine, speravi"

Tristitia obsedit me; magno et forti exercitu vallavit me;
occupavit cor meum; clamoribus et armis die noctuque contra
me pugnare non cessat. Amici mei sunt in castris eius et facti
sunt mihi inimici. Quaecumque video, quaecumque audio, vexilla tristitiae deferunt. Memoria amicorum me contristat;
recordatio filiorum me affligit; consideratio claustri et cellae me
angit; meditatio studiorum meorum dolore me afficit; cogitatio
peccatorum vehementer me premit. Sicut enim febre laborantibus
omnia dulcia amara videntur, ita mihi omnia in moerorem et
tristitiam convertuntur. Magnum profecto onus super cor tristitia
haec. Venenum aspidum, pestis pernitiosa, murmurat contra
Deum; blasphemare non cessat; ad desperationem hortatur.

Infelix ego homo! Quis me de manibus eius sacrilegis liberabit?
Si omnia quae video et audio vexilla sequuntur et fortiter contra
me pugnant, quis erit protector meus? Quis auxiliabitur mihi?
Quo vadam? Quo pacto effugiam? Scio quid faciam. Ad invisibilia
me convertam et adducam ea contra visibilia. Et quis erit dux
tam excelsi tamque terribilis exercitus? Spes, quae de invisibilibus
est. Spes, inquam, contra tristitiam veniet et expugnabit eam.
Quis stare poterit contra spem? Audi quid dicit Propheta: "Tu es,
Domine, spes mea; altissimum posuisti refugium tuum." Quis
stabit contra Deum? Quis expugnare poterit refugium eius, quod
est altissimum? Vocabo itaque eam: veniet profecto, nec me
confundet. Ecce iam venit; gaudia attulit; pugnare me docuit,
dixitque mihi: "Clama, ne cesses." Et aio: "Quid clamabo?" "Dic,"
inquit, "confidenter ex toto corde":

Exposition of the Psalm
"In You, O Lord, Have I Hoped"

Sadness besets me, has walled me round with a great and mighty army, has taken over my heart, and ceases not to fight against me day and night with shouts and arms. My friends are in her camp and have become my enemies. All that I see, all that I hear carry the banner of Sadness. Remembering my friends saddens me, recalling my children afflicts me, the thought of my cloister and cell brings me grief; reflection on my studies gives me pain; the thought of my sins weighs very heavily on me. Just as all sweet foods seem bitter to those in the grip of fever, so everything has been turned into woe and Sadness for me. This Sadness is indeed a heavy burden on my heart. The poison of asps, a deadly plague, murmurs against God and does not stop blaspheming; it counsels me to despair.

What an unhappy man am I! Who will free me from her sacrilegious hands? Who will be my protector, when all that I see and hear are following her banners and fighting strenuously against me? Who will come to my help? Where will I go? How can I flee? I know what I will do. I will turn to things invisible and lead them out against things visible. Who will be the leader of such a renowned and terrible army? Hope, which deals with the invisible. Hope, I say, will march against Sadness and take her by storm. Who shall be able to stand against Hope? Hear what the prophet says: "Lord, you are my hope; you have made the most high your refuge" [Ps 91:9]. Who will stand against God? Who will be able to take his refuge by storm, when it is the most high? I therefore call upon Hope. She will come indeed and will not confound me. See, she comes already and brings joy along. She taught me to fight and said to me, "Cry out and cease not" [Isa 58:1]. And I say, "What shall I cry?" She says, "Speak boldly with your whole heart."

"In te, Domine, speravi; non confundar in aeternum; in
iustitia tua libera me."

O mira potentia spei, cuius faciem non potuit tolerare tristitia!
Iam venit consolatio. Clamet et obstrepat cum exercitu suo nunc
tristitia. Premat mundus; insurgant hostes: nihil timeo, quoniam
in te, Domine, speravi; quoniam tu es spes mea; quoniam
altissimum posuisti refugium tuum. Iam ipsum ingressus sum:
spes me introduxit; non ego impudenter intravi; ipsa me excusabit
coram te. "Ecce," inquit spes, "O homo, altissimum refugium
Dei! Aperi oculos tuos et vide. Deus solus est; solus ipse est sub-
stantiae pelagus infinitum; caetera ita sunt ac si non essent: omnia
enim pendent ab eo, et, nisi sustentaret ea, in nihilum repente
redirent, quia ex nihilo facta sunt. Considera potentiam eius, qui
in principio creavit caelum et terram. Numquid non ipse omnia
in omnibus operatur? Quis potest movere manum sine eo? Quis
potest aliquid a se cogitare? Pensa sapientiam eius, qui in
tranquillitate omnia gubernat; qui omnia videt; 'cuius oculis omnia
sunt nuda et aperta.' Hic, hic est qui solus te liberare scit et potest,
solus consolari, solus salvare. 'Noli confidere in filiis hominum,
in quibus non est salus.' Cor hominis in manu eius: quocumque
voluerit, vertet illud. Hic est qui potest et scit te iuvare. An forte
tibi est suspecta voluntas? Pensa bonitatem eius; considera
dilectionem. An non ipse est amator hominum, qui pro hominibus
factus est homo et pro peccatoribus crucifixus? Hic vere est pater
tuus, qui te creavit, qui te redemit, qui tibi semper benefecit.
Numquid poterit pater relinquere filium suum? Proiice te in eum
et excipiet et salvabit te. Scrutare Scripturas et invenies quam
studiose tanta maiestas te monet ut speres in eum. Cur hoc?
Nempe quia salvare vult. Quid per Prophetam dicit? 'Quoniam
in me speravit, liberabo eum.' Ecce quia nulla alia causa liberare

"In you, O Lord, have I hoped; may I never be confounded; in your justice deliver me" [Ps 31:1].

O the wonderful power of Hope! Sadness could not bear her face. Consolation comes now. Let Sadness shout and drown out everything else with her army for now. The world weighs heavy, my enemies arise—I fear nothing because I have hoped in you, O Lord. Because you are my hope, because you have set up a lofty refuge for me. I have already entered it. Hope introduced me, I did not enter rudely, she will plea for me before you. Hope speaks: "See, O man, God's lofty refuge! Open your eyes and see. He alone is God, he alone is an infinite ocean of substance. Other things exist just as if they did not exist, for all things depend on him, and unless he upholds them, they instantly return into nothing because they were made from nothing. Reflect on the power of him who created heaven and earth at the beginning. Did he not himself cause everything in all things? Who can move a hand without him? Who can think anything by himself? Think about the wisdom of him who governs all things with tranquillity, who sees all things, 'to whose eyes all things are laid bare and open' [Heb 4:13]. He, he it is who alone knows how to deliver you and can do it; he alone can console you, he alone can save you. 'Do not trust in the children of humans, in whom there is no salvation' [Ps 145:3]. The human heart is in his hand; he may turn it in any direction he would want. He it is who has the power and knowledge to help you. Perhaps you have some doubt about his will? Ponder his goodness; think about his love. Does he not love everybody, he who became human for the sake of humans and was crucified for sinners? He is truly your Father, who created you, who redeemed you, who always benefitted you. Could a father desert his son? Throw yourself upon him, and he will catch you and save you. Search the Scriptures, and you will find how zealously his great majesty warns you to hope in him. Why so? Obviously because he wants to save you. What does he say through the Prophet? 'I will free him because he has hoped in me' [Ps

eum vult, nisi quia speravit in eum. Et quid prophetae, quid apostoli, quid denique ipse apostolorum Dominus praedicaverunt nisi ut homines in Domino sperarent? 'Sacrificate itaque, homines, sacrificium iustitiae, et sperate in Domino,' et ipse liberabit vos et eruet de omni tribulatione."

O magna virtus spei! Nimirum "diffusa est gratia in labiis tuis!" O vere altissimum refugium tuum, Domine, ad quod malum tristitiae accedere non poterit! Haec cognovi et intellexi: ideo in te, Domine, speravi. Quamquam enim peccatorum moles me graviter premat, tamen desperare nescio, quia bonitas tua tam benigne me ad sperandum provocat. Ideo non confundar in aeternum. Potero quidem in tempore confundi, non tamen in aeternum. Spes enim, quae me introduxit in altissimum refugium tuum, non me docuit sperare temporalia sed aeterna. Nam spes de invisibilibus est: "quae autem videntur temporalia sunt; quae vero non videntur, aeterna." Audiens itaque ego verba spei, quae me eripere de manibus tristitiae venit, in te, Domine, speravi, cupiens ante omnia a peccatis liberari et per misericordiam et gratiam tuam ad aeterna, quae non videntur, pervenire. Hoc primum desiderium meum. Mea enim peccata sunt mea maxima tribulatio: ab hac enim omnis alia tribulatio proficiscitur. Tolle, Domine, peccata mea et liber sum ab omni tribulatione, nam tribulatio et angustia de fonte cordis procedit: omnis enim tristitia ex amore provenit. Si amo filium et moritur, tribulor quia perdidi quod amabam; si servum non amo et moritur, non contristor, quia perdidi quod non amabam. Tolle ergo, Domine, peccata mea per gratiam tuam. Quid restat nisi ut te ex toto corde diligam et omnia temporalia ut vana contemnam? Si ergo te habeo per fidem, a quo etiam id spero "quod oculus non vidit nec auris audivit nec in cor hominis ascendit," quid me poterit conturbare? Quicquid praeter Deum amisero, perdidi quod non amo. In te

91:14]. See how he wishes to free him for no other reason except that he has hoped in him. What did the prophets, what did the apostles, what finally did the Lord of the apostles himself preach except that people should hope in the Lord? 'Offer therefore sacrifices of justice, O people, and hope in the Lord' [Ps 5:5], and he will free you and dig you out of all tribulation."

How great is the virtue of Hope! Indeed "grace has been poured forth on your lips" [Ps 45:2]. O truly most lofty refuge, O Lord, which the evil of Sadness will not be able to approach! This I knew and understood: I therefore have hoped in you, O Lord. Even though the mass of my sins weighs heavily upon me, still I know not how to despair because your goodness so graciously provokes me to go on hoping. Therefore I will not be confounded in eternity. Certainly in time I could be confounded, but not in eternity. For Hope, which has brought me into your lofty refuge has taught me not to hope in things temporal, but eternal. Hope deals with things not seen: "Things which are seen are temporal, things which are not seen are eternal" [2 Cor 4:18]. Hearing therefore words of Hope, who came to rescue me from the hands of Sadness, I hoped in you, O Lord; and desiring above all to be freed from sins and to attain through your mercy and grace the eternal things which are not seen. This is my first desire. My sins are my greatest tribulation: from it all the rest of my tribulation comes forth. Take away my sins, Lord, and I am free from all tribulation, for tribulation and anguish come from the fountain of the heart: for all sadness grows out of love. If I love my son and he dies, I am in sorrow because I lost what I loved. If I do not love my servant and he dies, I am not sad, because I lost what I did not love. Lord, take away my sins through your grace. What recourse remains, except that I love you with all my heart and spurn all things temporal as vain. If through faith I possess you, from whom I hope for that "which eye has not seen, ear has not heard, nor has it reached the human heart" [1 Cor 2:9], what will be able to cause me anxiety? When I shall have lost anything

itaque, Domine, speravi quomodo spes mea me sperare docuit:
ideo non confundar in aeternum, quia mihi dabis aeterna. Qui
autem non sperat in te, sed in vanitate sua, confundetur in
aeternum, quia ad aeternam confusionem descendet. Potero
quidem confundi temporaliter et a te et ab hominibus, sed non
confundar in aeternum. A te quippe, dum peto liberari ab angustia
temporali, et fortassis non exaudis me, confundor quidem tunc
temporaliter ut non confundar in aeternum: non enim expedit
mihi, "quia virtus in infirmitate perficitur." Ab hominibus vero
temporaliter confundor et praevalent adversum me quando
persequuntur me, sed hoc etiam permittitur a te ut in aeternum
non confundar. Si ergo ante te "mille anni sunt tamquam dies
hesterna quae praeteriit," confusiones temporales libenter
substinebo ut non confundar in aeternum. Sperabo in Domino
quomodo spes me sperare docet et cito ab omni tribulatione
liberabor. Quibus meritis liberabor? Non meis, Domine, sed in
iustitia tua libera me. In iustitia tua, dico, non mea. Ego enim
misericordiam quaero, non meam iustitiam offero. Sed, si per
gratiam tuam me iustum reddideris, iam habebo iustitiam tuam.
Gratia enim tua in nobis est iustitia tua. Pharisaei confidebant in
operibus iustitiae; confidebant quidem in iustitia sua, et ideo
iustitiae Dei non fuerunt subiecti, quia "ex operibus legis non
iustificabitur omnis caro coram Deo." Iustitia autem Dei apparuit
per gratiam Iesu Christi etiam sine operibus legis. Philosophi
gloriabantur in iustitia sua, et ideo non invenerunt iustitiam tuam,
quia non intrabant per ostium: fures erant et latrones, qui venerant
non ad salvandum sed ad perdendum et mactandum oves. Gratia
ergo tua iustitia tua, Domine; et gratia iam non esset gratia si ex
meritis daretur. Ergo non in iustitia mea, sed in iustitia tua, libera
me a peccatis meis: vel certe libera me in iustitia tua, idest in Filio
tuo, qui solus inter homines inventus est iustus. Quid ergo est

except God, I have lost what I do not love. I have hoped in you then, O Lord, as my Hope taught me to hope: hence I will not be confounded forever, because you will give me things eternal. He, however, who does not hope in you but in his own vanity, will be forever confounded, because he will go down to eternal confusion. I may be confounded for a time by you and by people, but I will not be confounded forever. You shame me then for a time when perchance you do not hear me when I ask to be delivered from temporal distress so that I may not be confounded forever. It was not good for me "because virtue is made perfect in weakness" [2 Cor 12:9]. Humans confound me for a time and prevail against me when they persecute me, but you also allow this so that I be not confounded forever. If in your sight "a thousand years are like yesterday which has passed on" [Ps 90:4], I will gladly bear temporal confusions so that I be not confounded forever. I will hope in God as Hope teaches me to hope, and I will be quickly delivered from all tribulation. By what merits will I be delivered? Not by my own merits, O Lord, but in your justice deliver me. In your justice, I say, not in my own. For I ask for mercy, I do not put forward my own justice. But if it is through your grace that you would have made me just, then I already have your justice. Your grace is your justice in us. The Pharisees trusted in works of justice, they trusted in their own justice, and therefore they were not included under God's justice because "no flesh will be justified before God by the works of the law" [Rom 3:20]. God's justice has appeared through the grace of Jesus Christ even without the works of the law. The philosophers boasted about their justice and so did not find your justice because they did not enter by the gate. They were thieves and robbers who came not to save but to destroy and slaughter the sheep. Your grace is your justice, Lord; and grace would not be grace if it were given because of merits. Therefore deliver me from my sins not in my justice but in your justice, or certainly deliver me in your justice, that is, in your Son, who alone among humans is found just.

Filius tuus nisi ipsa iustitia, in qua omnes homines iustificantur?
In tua ergo iustitia iustifica me et libera me a peccatis meis, ut
liberer etiam ab aliis tribulationibus quas propter ea patior, ut,
remota causa, removeatur effectus. Ecce te, Domine, rogavi et
consolatus sum! Spes ita me docuit. Gavisus sum quia in te,
Domine, speravi: ideo non confundar in aeternum.

Tristitia rediit; cum magno apparatu reversa est; gladiis et
lanceis undique munita est; magno impetu graditur; iam civitatem
nostram circumcinxit. Terruit me clamor equitum eius. Foris stans,
silentium indixit et procul locuta est: "O," inquit, "ecce qui
speravit in Domino, qui dixit: 'non confundar in aeternum,' qui
spem consolatricem secutus est!" Et, cum me ad haec verba
erubescere conspexit, appropians ait: "Ubi tuae spei promissa?
ubi consolatio? ubi liberatio? Quid tibi profuerunt lacrimae? Quid
orationes tuae tibi attulerunt de caelo? Clamasti et nemo respondit
tibi. Flevisti et quis, misericordia motus, est super te? Invocasti
Deum tuum et ipse tacuit. Rogasti eum et obsecrasti, et non fuit
vox neque sensus. Implorasti omnes sanctos et nullus eorum
respexit te. Ecce quid tibi attulerunt verba spei. Laborasti et nihil
in manibus tuis invenisti. An putas quia Deus haec inferiora
respiciat? 'Circa cardines caeli perambulat, nec nostra considerat.'"

Haec illa blasphemans aiebat et, cum ad verba eius
horrescerem, appropians, in aure locuta est. "Putas vera esse quae
fides praedicat? Vis videre ea hominum esse commenta? Vel ex
hoc cognosce: quia, si Deus factus esset homo et pro hominibus
crucifixus, non posset tanta pietas hominem, maximo moerore
confectum, ad se clamantem et lacrimantem, non consolari. Si,

What then is your Son, if not justice itself, in which all humans are justified? So justify me in your justice and deliver me from my sins in order that I may also be delivered from the other tribulations which I suffer because of my sins so that the effect may be removed after the cause has been removed. See Lord, I asked you, and I am consoled. Hope taught me this. I was made happy because I have hoped in you, Lord; therefore I will not be confounded forever.

Sadness has returned. She has come back with a large train; she is equipped all round with swords and spears. She advances in a powerful assault; she has already surrounded our city. The shouting of her cavalry terrified me. She stood outside and demanded silence and spoke from afar. She said, "See him who hoped in the Lord; who said, 'I will not be confounded forever,' who had found a consoler in Hope." When she spied me blushing at these words, she came up and said, "Where are those promises of your Hope? Where is consolation? Where deliverance? What good have your tears done you? What have your prayers brought you from heaven? You called out, and nobody answered you. You wept, and who was moved by pity to hover over you? You called upon your God, and he was silent. You asked him and beseeched him, and there was no voice, no sensation. You implored all the saints, and none of them paid attention to you. See what the words of Hope have brought you. You labored and found your hands empty. Do you think God pays attention to anything here below? 'He walks around the poles of heaven and does not worry about our affairs' [Job 22:14]."

She was mouthing these blasphemies, and when I shuddered at her words, she came up and spoke in my ear, saying: "Do you think that the things faith preaches are true? Do you want to see how they are human fabrications? Recognize it from this: because, if God had become man and had been crucified for human beings, such great kindness could not fail to console a person who was worn out by extreme distress and was crying out to

ut aiunt, bonitas infinita eum de caelo descendere fecit ut crucem
subiret, quomodo nunc ad homines miseros non descenderet ut
eos consolaretur? Hoc certe facilius est, et eadem pietate sub-
veniendum. Cur potius angeli et beati, si tam pii sunt, non ad te
consolandum veniunt? Quot putas homines, si possent, ad te
venirent et verbis ac operibus, quantum facultas daretur, te
laetificarent? Quot etiam ab omni angustia te liberarent? Cur hoc
non faciunt beati, qui longe meliores hominibus esse creduntur?
Mihi crede: casu omnia reguntur; non sunt nisi ea quae videntur;
spiritus noster evanescet sicut fumus. Quis unquam reversus ab
inferis nuntiavit aliquid de his quae dicuntur post mortem
animabus evenire? Fabulae sunt hae muliercularum. Surge, ergo,
et ad auxilia hominum confuge ut, de isto carcere solutus, taliter
vivas ut non frustra, ab ista tua spe deceptus, semper labores."

His dictis, tantus clamor auditus est in castris eius, tantus
armorum strepitus ac tubarum clangor ut vix subsistere potuerim,
et, nisi spes mea dilecta mihi auxilium praestitisset, vinctum catenis
me ad suam regionem tristitia deduxisset. Venit itaque spes, divino
quodam splendore corusca, et subridens dixit: "Eia, miles Christi!
Quid tibi cordis, quid tibi animi est in isto certamine?" Quod
audiens, illico erubui. Et illa: "Noli," inquit, "timere! Non capiet
te malum; nequaquam peribis. Ecce ego tecum sum ut liberem
te. An nescis quia scriptum est: 'Dixit insipiens in corde suo: non
est Deus'? Quasi una de stultis mulieribus locuta est tristitia haec.
Numquid tibi persuaderi poterit non esse Deum, aut Deum non
habere providentiam omnium? An poteris de fide dubitare, tu
qui tot argumentis et rationibus eam roborasti? Miror te adeo ex
verbis eius esse prostratum. Dic mihi, obsecro: num in corde tuo

himself and weeping. If, as they say, his infinite goodness caused him to come down from heaven to undergo the cross, would he not descend now to people in misery to console them? This is certainly easier and should be undertaken with the same kindness. Why rather don't the angels and saints, if they are so kind, come to console you? How many people, do you figure, would come to see you, if they could, and cheer you up with their words and actions in so far as they were given the chance? How many would free you from all distress? Why aren't the blessed doing this since they are thought to be far better than humans? Believe me: everything is ruled by chance. Nothing exists except the things which are seen. Our spirit passes away like smoke. Who has ever returned from the underworld and related anything about the things that are said to happen to souls after death? These are the tales of little old ladies. Arise then and take refuge in human help so that when you are released from this prison you may live in such wise that you will not always struggle in vain, deceived by this Hope of yours."

After these words were spoken, so much outcry was heard in her camp and so much clashing of arms and blaring of trumpets that I could barely stand it. Unless my beloved Hope had brought me help, Sadness would have led me off bound in chains to her realm. Hope came then, sparkling with a certain divine splendor and said with a smile, "Aha, soldier of Christ! What sort of heart, what frame of mind do you have for this battle?" I blushed the instant I heard this.

She said, "Don't fear! Evil is not going to take you captive, you're not going to die. See, I am with you to deliver you. Don't you know what is written, 'The fool says in his heart, there is no God' [Ps 14:1]? Sadness made these statements like some foolish woman. Could you have been persuaded that God does not exist or that he does not have providence of everything? Could you have doubts about the faith, you who have strengthened the faith with so many proofs and arguments? I am amazed that you were

de fide dubitare coepisti?" "Vivit Dominus et vivit anima tua, O mater mea dulcissima, quia nec minimum infidelitatis stimulum sensi: nam, per Christi gratiam, non minus credo vera esse quae fidei sunt quam ea quae oculis corporeis cerno. Verum tristitia adeo me premebat ut potius traherer ad desperationem quam ad infidelitatem." "Fili, scias hoc magnum donum esse Dei, 'nam fides donum Dei est, non ex operibus, ne quis glorietur.' Exurge, ergo, et noli timere: sed potius ex hoc cognosce quia non reliquit te Dominus, qui, si non cito exaudit, non est desperandum. 'Si moram fecerit, expecta eum, quia veniens veniet, et non tardabit.' Agricola patienter expectat fructum in tempore suo. Natura non statim introducit formam cum aliquid generat, sed primum materiam praeparat et paulatim disponit donec susceptioni fiat idonea. Scias, tamen, Dominum semper pie et humiliter orantes exaudire: nunquam enim ab eo vacui recedunt. Nec rationibus hoc probare contendam eo quod in te ipso hoc senseris. Dic mihi: quis cor tuum ad Deum levavit de terra? Quis te ad orandum perduxit? Quis dolorem peccatorum et lacrimas exibuit? Quis spem dedit? Quis te hilarem in oratione et post eam reliquit? Quis te in sancto proposito quotidie confirmavit? Nonne Dominus, qui omnia in omnibus operatur? Si igitur haec tibi iugiter dona largitur, cur dicit illa feminarum pessima: 'Ubi sunt orationes tuae? ubi lacrimae?' et caetera verba blasphemiae? An nescis quia distincta est caelestis Hierusalem ab ista terrestri? An ignoras quia nec conveniens nec necessarium nec item utile est Deum seu angelos et sanctos eius visibiliter ad homines descendere et eis familiariter loqui? Conveniens quippe non est propter distantiam meritorum. Quae, enim, conventio lucis ad tenebras? Non enim bene conveniunt viatores et comprehensores. Diversae

so bowled over by her words. Tell me, I ask: Did you begin to doubt about the faith in your heart?"

"God lives and your soul lives, O my sweet mother, because I felt not the least prompting to disbelief. For through Christ's grace I believe that the things which are of faith are no less true than the things I see with my bodily eyes. But Sadness pressed me so hard that I was being drawn more to despair than to disbelief."

"Son, you know that this is a great gift from God, 'for faith is a gift from God, it is not from works, lest anybody boast' [Eph 2:8-9]. Arise and fear not. Rather understand from this [experience] that the Lord will not desert you. There is no basis for despair if he does not speedily hear you. 'If he should delay, wait for him, he is coming and will come and will not be late' [Hab 2:3]. The farmer waits patiently for his crop at its own time. Nature does not instantly insert the form when it generates something; it prepares the prime matter and gradually makes it suitable until it is suited for taking on [its form]. But realize that the Lord always hears those who pray with reverence and humility. They never go away from him empty. I'm not going to attempt to prove by arguments what you feel is in yourself. Tell me: who raised your heart from the ground up to God? Who led you to pray? Who caused sorrow over your sins and tears? Who gave you hope? Who left you happy during prayer and after it? Who strengthened you daily in your holy determination? Was it not the Lord, who brings about everything in all beings? If he is constantly bestowing on you these gifts, why does that worst of women say: 'Where are your prayers? Where are your tears,' and her other words of blasphemy? Don't you know that the heavenly Jerusalem is different from this earthly one? Are you ignorant that it is not appropriate or necessary or even useful for God or his angels and saints to come down visibly to human beings and hold familiar conversations with them? It is not appropriate because of the disparity of merits. What do light and darkness have in common? Pilgrims

civitates diversos habent cives. Verum, quibusdam propter excellentiam sanctitatis, cum sint iam patriae vicini, datum est angelos videre et eos alloqui; sed speciale privilegium non omnes tangit. Necessarium autem non est, quia, cum invisibiliter beati nos gubernent et illuminent ac consolentur, non est opus visibiles apparitiones adhibere, quamquam Dominus adeo bonus est ut apparitiones etiam visibiles, cum opus fuerit, nunquam praetermittat. 'Quid enim potuit facere pro nostra salute et non fecit?' Utile quoque non est, quia nimia familiaritas parit contemptum: nam Judaeis miracula et magna et multa nihil profuerunt. Rara, enim, pretiosa sunt. Sufficiat ergo tibi invisibilis visitatio. Scit, enim, Dominus quid opus sit tibi. An non ipse consolatus est te? Scio quid in tuo corde sensisti. Surge, ergo, et ad orationem revertere! Clama, pete, quaere, pulsa, persevera, 'quia si non dabit eo quod amicus eius sis, propter importunitatem tamen dabit omnia quae tibi sunt necessaria.'"

His verbis consolatus, surrexi et, prostratus ante Deum, prosecutus sum orationem meam dicens:
"Inclina ad me aurem tuam; accelera ut eruas me."
Domine, Deus meus, ad te revertor! Spes me misit: non mea presumptione venio. Bonitas tua me invitat; misericordia tua me trahit. O quanta dignatio! Gaudeo plane; nec alia mihi superest consolatio. Felix profecto ista necessitas, quae me ad Deum venire compellit; quae me cogit loqui cum eo; quae me urget orare. Loquar igitur ad Deum meum, quamvis sim pulvis et cinis. Inclina, Domine, aurem tuam! Quid ais, anima mea? Num Deus habet aures? Num ipse corpus est? Absit. Cum enim longe melior sit spiritus corpore, quis asserat Deum esse corpus nisi insanus? Sed balbutiendo, ut possumus, excelsa tua, Domine, resonamus. Cognoscimus te per creaturas; loquimur tibi et de te per earum similitudines. Auris itaque tua, Domine, quid est? an forte cognitio

and those who have reached the goal are not yet together. Different communities have different citizens. Admittedly it has been granted to some persons because of their pre-eminent holiness to see and speak with angels when they are already close to their fatherland, but a special privilege does not apply to all. It is not necessary because, since the blessed govern and enlighten and console us invisibly, there is no need to employ visible apparitions, although the Lord is so good that he never fails to provide visible apparitions also, should there be need. 'What could he have done for our salvation and has not done' [Isa 5:4]? It is not useful because too much familiarity breeds contempt, for the Jews derived no profit from his many great miracles. Rare objects are precious. An invisible visitation is enough for you. God knows what you need. Did he not console you himself? I know what you felt in your heart. Arise then and return to prayer. Cry out, entreat, request, knock, persevere, 'because if he will not give because he is his friend, because of the importunity he will still give everything you need' [Luke 11:8]."

Consoled by these words I arose and lying prostrate before God continued with my prayer, saying:

"Bend your ear to me, hurry to rescue me" [Ps 31:2].

Lord, my God, I am coming back to you! Hope sent me; I do not come on my own presumption. Your goodness invites me, your mercy draws me. What enormous graciousness! I am quite delighted. No other consolation remains for me. This is truly a happy necessity which forces me to come to God, which drives me to talk with him, which pushes me to pray. So let me talk with my God, even though I am dust and ashes. Bend your ear, Lord! My soul, what are you saying? Does God have ears? Does he have a body? Far from it. Since a spirit is far superior to a body, who but a madman would assert that God is a body? Lord, we echo your greatness as best we can with our stammering. We know you through your creatures, we speak to you and about you using

tua? Nam per aures intelligimus ea quae nobis dicuntur: tu, autem, omnia quae loquuntur et cogitant homines ab aeterno cognovisti. Num ergo per aurem tuam accipere possumus cognitionem tuam? Aliquid profecto insinuat mihi auris tua, quod non capitur in nomine simplicis cognitionis tuae. Nam quibusdam inclinas aurem tuam, ab aliis vero avertis eam: cognitio autem tua semper eadem permanet. Quid, ergo, auris tua nisi approbationis et reprobationis notitia tua? Inclinas aurem tuam et audis verba iustorum, quia tibi placent et approbas ea. Avertis aurem tuam a verbis impiorum, quia ab impietate recedere nolunt, quia tibi non placent et reprobas ea. Quid est, ergo, inclinare aurem tuam loquentibus tibi nisi eorum orationes approbare et eos, vultu pietatis, aspicere, illuminare et accendere, ut cum fiducia et caritatis fervore te orent, teque deprecentur, quia eis dare vis quod humili pietate postulant? Nam si rex pauperi, cupienti loqui cum eo, vultum hilarem ostendat, oculos ad eum convertat et attentum verbis eius se demonstret, nonne laetabitur pauper? Nonne facies et attentio regis eloquium ei praestabit? Nonne verba et facundiam subministrabit? Ita, Domine, intelligimus, te ad nostras preces tunc inclinare aurem tuam quando nos in oratione spiritu fervere concedis. Rogo, ergo, te, Domine: inclina ad me aurem tuam; approba orationem meam; illumina me; accende me; doce quid petere debeam; eleva sursum cor meum ut tandem exaudias deprecationem meam; accelera ut eruas me; abbrevia dies; festina tempus. Ita inclina ad me aurem tuam ut cito merear exaudiri. Tibi, enim, qui habitas aeternitatem, omne tempus breve est: aeternitas namque tota simul comprehendit et in immensum excedit totum tempus universum. At mihi quaelibet dies longa est, nam tempus est numerus motus. Qui, enim, motum non

them metaphorically. What then, Lord, is your ear? Perhaps your knowledge? We understand what is said to us through our ears; but you have known from eternity all that humans say and think. Is it through your ear that we can come to your knowledge? Your ear suggests something to me which does not come under the name of simple knowledge of you. For you bend your ear to certain people but turn it away from others. But your knowledge always remains the same. What is your ear, therefore, except your taking note with approval and disapproval? You bend your ear and hear the words of the just, because they please you and you approve of them. You turn your ear away from the words of the wicked, because they do not want to leave their wickedness behind, because their words do not please you and you reject them. What does it mean, then, to bend your ear to those who are speaking to you except that you approve of their prayers and look upon, enlighten, and inflame them with your kindly countenance so that they pray to you with confidence and the fervor of love and beseech you that you be willingly to give them what they request with humble kindness?

If a king shows a smiling face to a poor man who desires to speak with him, if he turns his eyes to him and shows that he is paying attention to his words, does not the poor man rejoice? Don't the face and attention of the king lend him eloquence? Don't they enhance his words and fluency? In the same way, Lord, we understand that you are then bending your ear to our prayers when you grant us to be spiritually fervent in prayer. So I ask you, Lord, bend your ear to me, approve of my prayer, enlighten me, set me afire, teach me what I should be asking for, lift up my heart so that you may at last listen to my petition, hasten to rescue me, shorten the days, hurry up time. So bend your ear to me that I may quickly merit being heard. For you, who dwell in eternity, all time is short; for eternity embraces all time in a single moment and stretches immeasurably beyond all time. But for me, every day is long, for time is the measure of motion. The

sentit nec tempus quidem sentit; et qui sentit motum et tempus sentit. Maxime autem motum sentit qui numerat partes eius. Ego, itaque, quia numero dies et horas, maxime tempus sentio: et ideo, sicut tibi "mille anni tamquam dies hesterna quae praeteriit," ita mihi una dies tamquam mille anni qui venturi sunt. Accelera, ergo, Domine, ut eruas me a peccatis et adversitatibus meis, nam mors properat et in omni loco me expectat. Accelera, Domine, ne forte, praeoccupatus ab ea, non habeam spatium paenitentiae. Erue me, Domine, de manu maligni. Libera me de vinculis peccati. Eripe me de laqueo mortis. Educ me de profundo inferni. Salva me ab oppressione et dura servitute tristitiae, ut anima mea exurgat et laetetur in te et benedicat tibi omnibus diebus vitae suae. Gratias tibi, Domine, per Iesum salvatorem meum, quia "secundum multitudinem dolorum meorum in corde meo, consolationes tuae laetificaverunt animam meam." Ego, igitur, semper in te sperabo et adiciam super omnem laudem tuam. Tu, autem, Domine, inclina ad me aurem tuam; accelera ut eruas me.

Heu, me miserum! Ecce iterum tristitia terribilibus armis instructa! Vexillum iustitiae praecedit eam. Innumerabilis exercitus sequitur pedes eius. Unusquisque lanceam habet in manu sua. Vasa mortis circumquaque conspicio. Vae mihi, quia perii! Voce horribili clamat: "O miser, spes illa tua te decepit! Ecce, laborasti in vanum! Dixisti enim: 'Inclina ad me aurem tuam; accelera ut eruas me.' Numquid inclinavit ad te Deus aurem suam? Numquid exaudita est oratio tua? Ubi liberatio? ubi consolatio? Num acceleravit eruere te? Adhuc vinctus es: nihil erga te innovatum est. Si credis fidem esse veram, cur spem solam amplecteris? An nescis quia Deus iustus est? An ignoras iustitias eius? Angelis suis non pepercit; non misertus est eis, neque miserebitur: propter unum peccatum tantum damnati sunt in perpetuum. Adam peccavit et iustitia Dei totum genus humanum morte punivit. An putas Deum non ita amare iustitiam sicut misericordiam?

person who does not feel motion does not feel time either. The
person who feels motion also feels time. The person who counts
its parts feels motion the most. I then feel time the most because
I count the days and hours, and so just as for you "a thousand
years are as yesterday which has passed" [Ps 90:4], so for me one
day is like a thousand years which are to come. Hurry, Lord, to
rescue me from sin and my enemies, for death hastens and waits
for me everywhere. Hurry, Lord, lest death take hold of me before I have room for repentance. Rescue me, Lord, from the hand
of an evil person. Deliver me from the chains of sin. Rescue me
from the snare of death. Lead me out of the depth of hell. Save
me from oppression and the harsh slavery of Sadness, so that my
soul may arise and rejoice in you and bless you all the days of my
life. Thanks be to you, Lord, through Jesus my Savior, because
"in accord with the multitude of the sufferings in my heart your
consolations have made glad my soul" [Ps 94:19]. Always then
will I hope in you, and I will add to all your praises. But you,
Lord, bend your ear to me; hurry to rescue me.

Alas, wretched me! See, Sadness is outfitted again with terri-
fying armaments. The banner of justice goes before her. A countless army follows in her footsteps. Each of them has a lance in his
hand. I spy the vessels of death everywhere. Woe is me, for I am
dying! Sadness cries out with a horrid voice, "O wretch, that Hope
of yours has betrayed you! See how you have labored in vain. You
said, 'Bend your ear to me, hurry to rescue me.' Did God ever
bend his ear to you? Was your prayer ever heard? Where is your
deliverance? Where your consolation? Did he hurry to rescue you?
You are still chained; nothing new has happened to you. If you
believe your faith is true, why are you embracing Hope alone?
Don't you know that God is just? Are you ignorant of his acts of
justice? He did not spare his angels; he has not taken pity of them
and will not take pity. For just one sin they were damned forever.
Adam sinned, and the justice of God punished the whole human
race with death. Do you think that God does not love justice just

Pueri, in originali peccato decedentes, nunquam videbunt faciem
Dei. Adeo, enim, severa est iustitia Dei ut, propter peccatum quod
ipsi non fecerunt sed contraxerunt, aeterna poena plectantur. In
inferno, autem, nulla est redemptio. Nescis quia Deus non parcit
delinquenti? Nonne tempore Noe perdidit fere totum genus humanum? Nonne Sodomam et reliquas civitates ei adhaerentes igne
consumpsit? Nec iustitia divina infantibus et innocentibus saltem
compassa est. Quotiens Judaeos peccantes punivit? Nonne
Hierusalem per manum Nabuchodonosor funditus evertit?
Templo quoque suo non pepercit. Quod etiam a Tito,
Romanorum principe, factum est: ubi tam crudeli animadversione
gravati sunt Judaei ut nemo sit qui audiens non expavescat. Sed
vide quam dura sit iustitia divina: filii pro patribus usque in
hodiernam diem puniuntur. Ecce, Judaei ubique terrarum servi
sunt et, in caecitate sua morientes, poenis cruciantur aeternis. An
putas quia maior sit misericordia Dei quam eius iustitia? Equidem
in ipso Deo neque maior neque minor est. Quicquid enim est in
Deo, est substantia eius. Sed opera iustitiae et misericordiae
consideremus. Nimirum opera iustitiae excedunt opera
misericordiae. Dominus ipse testis est, qui ait: 'multi sunt vocati,
pauci vero electi.' Pensa, obsecro, quot infideles damnantur, quot
mali christiani; quam pauci bene vivunt, et facile intelliges longe
plura esse vasa iustitiae quam misericordiae. Electi enim a Deo
vasa sunt misericordiae; reprobi, vero, vasa iustitiae. Non te sperare
faciat Maria Magdalena, non latro, non Petrus, non Paulus. Maria,
enim, una fuit, latro unus, Petrus unus, Paulus item unus. An
putas te inter paucos esse numerandum, qui tot et tam gravia
peccata commisisti, qui scandalum in Ecclesia fuisti, qui caelum
et terram offendisti? Ecce flevit oculus tuus; cor tuum
misericordiam semper imploravit et adhuc non es misericordiam
consecutus. Tot orationes eorum qui diligebant te, non fuerunt

as much as mercy? Children who go down in original sin will never see the face of God. So harsh is God's justice that they are punished with eternal punishment for a sin which they have not committed but contracted. But in hell there is no redemption. Are you ignorant that God does not spare those who go astray? Did he not punish almost the whole human race at the time of Noah? Did he not consume in fire Sodom and the other cities belonging to it? Neither did divine justice at least take pity on infants and innocent people. How often did he punish the Jews when they sinned? Did he not utterly destroy Jerusalem by the hand of Nebuchadnezzar? He also did not spare his own temple. That was done by Titus, a Roman prince, when the Jews were loaded with such severe punishment that there is nobody who is not terrified by hearing about it. But see how harsh is divine justice: sons are punished for their fathers right up to today. See how the Jews are slaves all over the earth, and dying in their blindness are tortured with eternal punishments.

Do you think that God's mercy is greater than his justice? Indeed in God himself it is neither greater nor lesser. Everything that is in God is his substance. But let us reflect on his works of justice and mercy. His works of justice indeed outnumber his works of mercy. The Lord himself is witness; he says, 'Many are called but few are chosen' [Matt 22:14]. Consider, I beg you, how many unbelievers are damned, how many bad Christians; how few live rightly, and you will easily understand that there are far more vessels of justice than of mercy. Those elected by God are the vessels of mercy, but the reprobate are the vessels of justice. Don't let Mary Magdalene cause you to have hope, nor the thief, nor Peter, nor Paul. Mary was one woman, the thief was one man, Peter one and Paul one as well. Do you think that you should be counted among the few, you who have committed so many and such grave sins, who were a scandal in the Church, who offended against heaven and earth? See, your eye shed tears; your heart always begged for mercy, but you have not yet re-

exauditae. Quare hoc? Nimirum quia inter vasa iustitiae computaris. Spes illa tua frustra te laborare fecit. Sequere consilium meum. Caelum te respuit; terra te non recipit. Confusionem hanc magnam quis tolerare possit? Melius est tibi mori quam vivere. Elige mortem, quam si nullus infert, mitte tu manus in te ipsum."

Haec illa, mira importunitate, ingerebat, totusque exercitus eius magnis vocibus congeminabat, dicens: "Mors sola refugium tuum! Mors sola refugium tuum!" Ego vero, haec audiens, expavi, et illico in faciem cecidi, eiulans et dicens: "Domine, adiuva me; Domine, ne derelinquas me! Spes mea, veni! Spes mea, veni!"

Ecce subito spes de caelo micans descendit, et tetigit latus meum, et levavit me, statuitque supra pedes meos, et ait: "Usquequo parvulus eris? Quamdiu tirunculus esse voles? Totiens in bello fuisti et in medio umbrae mortis ambulasti, et nondum certare didicisti? Noli, noli turbari de magna iustitia Dei! Confortare, pusillanimis! Timeant qui ad Dominum non convertuntur, qui ambulant in viis suis, qui sequuntur vanitates, qui viam pacis non cognoverunt. Paveant impii, qui peccant et dicunt: 'Quid feci?', qui non convertuntur ad cor, qui vocantur et venire renuunt, qui ignorant Deum et 'nolunt intelligere ut bene agant.' Hi ergo timeant quod dicit Apostolus: 'Horrendum est incidere in manus Dei viventis.' Tales profecto iustitia Dei punit: huiuscemodi homines ad eam spectant. At peccatores qui, ad se reversi, surgunt et ad patrem misericordiarum currunt, dicentes: 'Pater, peccavi in caelum et coram te, sed propitius esto mihi peccatori,' confidant in Domino, quia qui eos traxit, procul dubio suscipiet et iustificabit. Proferat in medium haec ipsa tristitia, si potest, aliquem peccatorem quantumlibet magnum, qui ad Dominum conversus sit et non fuerit ab eo susceptus et

ceived mercy. All the prayers of those who loved you have not been heard. Why so? Undoubtedly because you are numbered among the vessels of justice. That Hope of yours made you labor in vain. Follow my advice. Heaven has rejected you; the earth does not receive you. Who could put up with this great confusion? It is better for you to die than to live. Chose death. If nobody inflicts it, lay hands on yourself."

She kept pressing these arguments with wonderful persistence, and her whole army roared out together at the top of their voices, saying, "Death is your only recourse! Death is your only recourse!" Hearing this I was struck with fear and immediately fell on my face, shrieked, and said, "Lord, help me; Lord, do not desert me! My Hope, come! My Hope, come!"

Look, Hope suddenly darted forth and came from heaven. She touched my side and lifted me up and set me on my feet and said, "Are you going to be such a little child? How long do you want to remain a raw recruit? So many times you were in war and walked amidst the shadow of death, and you haven't yet learned how to fight? Don't worry, don't, about the great justice of God! Buck up, faint of heart! Let them fear who are not converted to God, who walk in their own ways, who chase after vanities, who do not know the path of his peace. Let the wicked fear, who sin and say, 'What have I done?' They are not converted in their heart, they are called but refuse to come, they ignore God, and 'do not want to know how to do good' [Ps 36:3]. Let those fellows fear what the Apostle says, 'It is a fearsome thing to fall into the hands of the living God' [Heb 10:31]. Truly it is such fellows that God's justice punishes; let such people watch out for it. But the sinners who come to themselves, rise up, run to the Father of mercies, and say, 'Father, I have sinned against heaven and before you' [Luke 15:21], but 'be merciful to me a sinner' [Luke 18:13], who trust in the Lord because he who has put up with them will undoubtedly receive and justify them. Let Sadness herself bring forth right up front, if she can, one sinner, however great, who

iustificatus. Quamvis, enim, de Esau scriptum sit: 'Non invenit
paenitentiae locum, quamquam cum lacrimis inquisisset eam,'
tamen hoc non obstat nostrae sententiae, quia Esau non flevit
propter peccata commissa, sed propter bona temporalia amissa,
quae recuperare non potuit. Nec putes iustitiam ita respicere
impios ut a misericordia penitus separetur; nec misericordiam ita
ad iustos spectare ut a iustitia seiungatur: 'universae,' enim, 'viae
Domini, misericordia et veritas.' Nam et peccatoribus
misericordiam facit dum eis, propter bona quae temporaliter
agunt, temporalia dona retribuit, et post hanc vitam eos, non
quantum merentur, punit; electos quoque sua iustitia prosequitur
dum, pro culpis, temporaliter eos affligit, ne poenis deputentur
aeternis. Tu, igitur, patienter interim substine Dominum: peccasti
enim. Paenitentiam age: sufficiat tibi remissio culpae per gratiam.
'Fili mi, noli negligere disciplinam Domini, neque fatigeris dum
ab eo argueris.' 'Quem enim diligit, Deus castigat.' Flagellat autem
omnem filium quem recipit. Persevera, ergo, in disciplina:
tamquam filio tibi offert se Deus. Et, quamvis pauci sint electi,
comparatione eorum qui reprobi sunt, innumerabiles tamen sunt
qui salvantur. Nec enim una est tantum Maria Magdalena, nec
tantum unus latro, unus Petrus, unus Paulus, quin innumerabiles
secuti sunt eorum vestigia paenitentiam agentes, et a Domino
suscepti et multis magnisque gratiae muneribus decorati. Nec
minor est misericordia in operibus suis quam iustitia, nam tam
magna dona misericordia iustis praestat, ut opera eius opera
iustitiae in immensum excedant. An nescis quia 'misericordia
Domini plena est terra'? Quaenam creatura potest gloriari se
aliquid habere et non accepisse illud a misericordia? Si, autem,
graviter Deum offendisti, maior est eius misericordia quam omnia
peccata mundi. Noli turbari propter multitudinem et gravitatem
peccatorum. Nonne misericordia iam occurrit tibi? Nonne

turned to the Lord and was not received by him and justified.
Even though it is written about Esau that 'he did not find an
opportunity for repentance, although he sought one with tears'
[Heb 12:17], still that does not contradict our statement because
Esau wept not because of the sins he committed but because of
the temporal goods he lost, which he could not recover.

"Don't think that justice is so aimed at the wicked that it is
kept completely separate from mercy, nor that mercy is so aimed
at the just that it is cut off from justice: 'All the paths of the Lord
are mercy and truth' [Ps 25:10]. For he has mercy on sinners
when he rewards them with temporal goods for the good they do
in time, and after this life he punishes them not as much as they
deserve. He also treats the elect with his justice when he afflicts
them for a time for their faults lest they be assigned to eternal
punishments. Meanwhile make yourself subject to the Lord in
patience, for you have sinned. Do penance; the remission of your
fault through grace is enough for you. 'My son, do not neglect
the discipline of the Lord and do not grow weary when you are
reproved by him' [Heb 12:5]. 'God chastises those whom he loves'
[Prov 3:12]. He scourges every son that he receives. Persevere in
his discipline: God is offering himself to you as to a son. Although few are elected compared to those who are rejected, still
those who are saved are beyond count. There is not just one Mary
Magdalene, nor only one thief, one Peter, one Paul; rather countless people have followed their footsteps and done penance, and
the Lord received them and bestowed on them many great gifts
of grace. His mercy toward his works is not less than his justice,
for his mercy grants such great gifts to the just that his works [of
mercy] immeasurably surpass his works of justice. Don't you know
that 'the earth is full of the Lord's mercy' [Ps 33:5]. What creature can boast about having something which it did not receive
from his mercy? But if you have seriously offended God, his mercy
is greater than all the sins of the world. Do not become anxious
about the multitude and gravity of your sins. Has his mercy not

osculata est te? Ecce, cecidisti et non es collisus. Quare? Numquid tu non es vas fragile quod, cum ceciderit, conteratur necesse est, nisi quis supponat manum suam? Quare, ergo, cadens, non es contritus? Quis supposuit manum suam? Quis, inquam, nisi Dominus? Signum hoc magnum electionis tuae! Electus, enim, 'cum ceciderit, non collidetur, quia Dominus supponet manum suam.' Nonne scribit Apostolus: 'Diligentibus Deum omnia cooperantur in bonum,' et adeo omnia ut etiam ipsum peccatum eis cooperetur in bonum? Nonne eis ille casus cooperatur in bonum, unde et humiliores efficiuntur et cautiores? Nonne Dominus cadentem illum suscipit, qui ab humilitate suscipitur? Dilexisti Dominum: pluribus annis pro eius amore laborasti. Elevasti deinde cor tuum, et 'in vanitate sensus tui ambulasti.' Subtraxit Dominus manum et cecidisti, et in profundum maris descendisti. Verumtamen dignatio Domini statim supposuit manum et non es collisus. Dic ergo: 'Impulsus, eversus sum ut caderem, et Dominus suscepit me.' Non sic impii; non sic quos Deus reprobavit. Cadentes enim non adiicient ut resurgant, sed aut pudore noxio excusant peccata, aut fit eis frons meretricis, et iam nec Deum timent nec hominem reverentur. Surge, itaque, et forti animo esto! 'Confortare, et esto robustus.' 'Expecta Dominum, et viriliter age: confortetur cor tuum, et substine Dominum.' Probasti virtutem tuam quam nulla sit. 'Humiliare iam sub potenti manu Dei,' et amodo cautior esto. Patientia tibi necessaria est. Sine intermissione ora, et Dominus exaudiet te in tempore opportuno. Surge, itaque, et omnem tristitiam a te repelle. Pedes Domini amplectere, et ipse liberabit et salvabit te."

run to meet you already? Has it not kissed you? See, you have fallen and are not smashed. Why? Are you not a fragile vase, which necessarily would break after it has fallen unless somebody put a hand under it? How come you, in falling, were not broken? Who put his hand under you? Who, I ask, except the Lord? This is a great sign of your election! One of the elect, 'should he have fallen, is not smashed because the Lord puts his hand under him' [Ps 37:24]. Did not the Apostle write, 'For those who love God, all things work together unto good' [Rom 8:28], all things to the point that for them even sin itself works together unto their good? Does not their falling work together unto good for them, so that from it they may be made more humble and careful? Does not the Lord receive the falling person who has been overtaken by humility? You have loved the Lord: many years have you worked out of love for him. You then became haughty of heart and 'walked in the futility of your mind' [Eph 4:17]. God withdrew his hand, and you fell and sank down into the depths of the sea. But suddenly the condescendence of the Lord interposed a hand, and you were not smashed. Say then, 'I was driven and overturned so that I might fall, and the Lord received me' [Ps 118:13]. Not so the wicked, not those whom the Lord has rejected. When they fall, they do not count on rising again, but either they make excuses for their sins with guilty shame, or they put on the face of a prostitute and then neither fear God nor respect men. Get up then and be of good heart! 'Take courage and be strong' [Josh 1:6]. 'Wait for the Lord and act bravely; may your heart take courage; wait for the Lord' [Ps 27:14]. You have tested your strength, how it is nothing. 'Humble yourself now under God's mighty hand' [Gen 16:9], and be more careful from now on. You need to have patience. Pray without ceasing, and the Lord will hear you at the proper time. Rise up then, and rid yourself of all sadness. Embrace the Lord's feet, and he will deliver you and save you."

His dictis, rapta est in caelum, me confortatum et miro modo consolatum relinquens. Quam statim ex toto corde prosecutus, ante Deum steti, et ad pedes mei Salvatoris provolutus, confidenter dixi:

"Esto mihi in Deum protectorem et in domum refugii, ut salvum me facias."

Tu enim, Deus, omnium magnus et fortissimus; tu redemptor et salvator universorum; tu protector tuorum fidelium! Ad te confugio confidenter! Spes me introduxit: spes, quam tua pietate summe diligis, quam nobis semper commendasti. Non timui ante faciem tuam cum ea venire. Fateor: indignus sum, sed ipsa me traxit. Timebam ingredi propter multa scelera mea, sed ipsa mihi fiduciam praebuit. Ecce, stat coram te: ipsa testimonium perhibeat. Loquar ad Dominum meum, caro et peccator. Spes me docuit, dixitque mihi ut confidenter os meum aperiam: "Dulcis," inquit, "est Dominus: non te repellet; non irascetur; libenter audiet; quicquid petieris, dabit." "Credidi ei: propter quod locutus sum." Verum, tuam maiestatem considerans, "humiliatus sum nimis, et dixi in excessu meo: omnis homo mendax." Non confidam in homine in aeternum, sed in te solo, quia tu solus fidelis in omnibus verbis tuis: omnis autem homo mendax. "Quid retribuam tibi, Domine, pro omnibus quae retribuisti mihi? Calicem salutaris accipiam," quia amodo non mihi sed tibi vivam. Pro tuo amore benefaciens, omnia mala tolerabo. Non mea virtute hoc faciam, "sed nomen Domini invocabo. Vota mea reddam coram omni populo tuo, quia pretiosa est in conspectu Dei mors sanctorum eius." Esto ergo mihi in Deum protectorem. Defende me ab inimicis meis. Inimici mei sunt peccata mea, quae iustitiam tuam provocant contra me. Non potero stare contra eam, nisi protegas me. Misericordia tua sit scutum meum, Domine, "ut scuto bonae voluntatis tuae corona me." Non habeo quid offeram

Having said these things, Hope was swept up into heaven, leaving me strengthened and consoled in a wonderful way. Right after following her with my whole heart, I stood before God and rushing to the feet of my Savior, I said with confidence:

"Be for me a God who protects and a house of refuge so that you may save me" [Ps 31:3].

You, God, are the greatest and strongest of all beings; you are the Redeemer and Savior of all things; you are the protector of your believers! I fly trustfully to you for refuge! Hope introduced me: Hope, whom you love supremely in your kindness, which you have always recommended to us. I did not fear to come before your face with her. I confess that I am unworthy, but she drew me along. I was fearful of entering because of my many crimes, but she gave me confidence. See how she stands before you, let her give testimony. Flesh and a sinner, I speak to my God. Hope coached me, she told me to open my mouth with confidence. "The Lord is sweet," she said. "He won't drive you away or get angry. He will hear you willingly and give you whatever you ask for." "I believed her, that is why I spoke" [Ps 116:10ff.]. But reflecting on your majesty, "I was greatly humiliated, and I said in my rapture, 'every man is a liar'" [Ps 116:10-11]. Never will I trust in man but in you alone because you are the only one who is faithful to all your statements. Every man is a liar. "What shall I give back to you, Lord, for all that you have given me? I will take up the chalice of salvation," because from now on I am going to live for you and not for me. Doing good out of love for you, I will bear with every evil. I will not do this by my own strength, "but I will call upon the name of the Lord. I will fulfill my vows before all your people because the death of his saints is precious in God's sight." Be then for me a God who protects. Defend me against my enemies. My enemies are my sins, which have called forth your justice against me. I will be unable to stand against your justice unless you protect me. Your mercy is my shield, Lord, "so that you may crown me with the

ei, quo furorem eius temperare possim. Omnia, quae mecum
porto, me accusant. Offeram ergo te, Domine! Ne indigneris,
Domine meus, sed magis esto mihi in Deum protectorem. Sub
alis tuis protege me; "scapulis tuis obumbra me, et sub pennis
tuis" sperabo. Quid faciet mihi iustitia si sub tua protectione me
custodies? Obmutescet, Domine; et gladium furoris sui reportabit
in locum suum; mitis efficietur, videns pietatem incarnationis
tuae, conspiciens vulnera passionis tuae, cernens sanguinem
caritatis tuae: recedet a me et dicet: "Laetare, fili: invenisti me;
comede; 'in pace in idipsum dormi et requiesce.'" Esto itaque,
Domine, mihi in Deum protectorem et in domum refugii, ut,
tempore pluviarum et procellarum, tempore temptationum,
confugiam ad te, quia in te solo salus mea. Sis mihi tu domus
refugii. Aperi mihi latus tuum lancea perforatum, ut ingrediar
pectus tantae pietatis, in quo salvus sim a pusillanimitate spiritus
et tempestate. Absconde me in tabernaculo tuo; in die malorum
protege me in abscondito tabernaculi tui. Sit domus refugii mei
ineffabilis pietas tua, ut salvum me facias. Non enim potero non
salvus esse in domo refugii tui: altissimum, enim, posuisti refugium tuum. Munitus est locus iste: nullus ibi timetur hostis.
Utinam semper in eo manere liceret! Qui habitat in eo, vulnerari
non potest. Ad omnem, igitur, temptationem, ad omnem
tribulationem, ad omnem denique cuiuscumque modi
necessitatem, aperi mihi, Domine, domum refugii tui; expande
sinum pietatis tuae; pateant viscera misericordiae tuae, ut salvum
me facias. Non accedet illuc temptator; non calumniator ascendet;
non pessimus fratrum accusator attinget: securus ero, et iam paene
mihi videor securus. Gratias tibi, bone Iesu, quia spem tuam ad

shield of your good will" [Ps 5:12]. I have nothing to offer justice, so that I might be able to temper its furious anger. Everything that I carry with me accuses me. Therefore I offer you, O Lord! Do not grow angry, my Lord, but be even more for me a God who protects. Protect me under your wings; "Cover me with your pinions, and under your wings" [Ps 91:4] will I hope.

What will justice do to me if you will guard me under your protection? It will fall silent, Lord, and will return the sword of its wrath to its place. It will become meek when it sees the kindness of your incarnation, when it understands the wounds of your passion, when it discerns the blood of your charity. It will back away from me and say, "Rejoice, son; you have found me. Dine with me, and 'in the peace of the same, sleep and take your rest'" [Ps 4:8].

Be then, Lord, for me a God who protects and a house of refuge so that in the time of rain and storm, in the time of temptation, I may take refuge in you, because you alone are my salvation. Be for me a house of refuge. Open to me your side pierced by the lance so that I may come into that breast of such kindness, in which I may be safe from the storm and the faintheartedness of my spirit. Hide me in your tabernacle, in the day of woe protect me in a hidden nook of your tabernacle. May your ineffable kindness be the house of my refuge so that you give me salvation. It will be impossible for me to be unsafe in the house of your refuge, for you have perched your refuge most high. It is a fortified place; no enemy is feared there. Would that one were allowed to stay in it forever! The person who dwells there cannot be hurt. Open to me, Lord, the house of your refuge against every temptation, against every tribulation, and finally against every need of whatever sort. Expand the breast of your kindness. May your merciful heart be opened so that you give me salvation. The tempter will not have access to it, the false accuser will not climb up, the most evil accuser of his brothers will not get in; I will be secure, and I am almost at the point of seeing myself as

me misisti, quae me de pulvere suscitavit et de stercore erexit, statuitque coram te, ut sis mihi in Deum protectorem et in domum refugii, ut salvum me facias.

Anima mea conturbata est! En adest tristitia! Cum vexillo iustitiae venit; ab hesterno conflictu non recedit; aliis tamen armis munita est, nam hac nocte arma mihi subripuit, gladiisque meis milites suos accinxit. Inermis, ergo, et infirmus, quid faciam? En quam procaciter clamat; quanto impetu me aggreditur; quantum confidit de victoria! "Ubi," inquit, "est protector tuus? ubi domus refugii? ubi salus? Adhuc permanes in fiducia tua vana? Consolationes illae tuae de tua imaginatione procedunt. Fingis tibi Deum propitium et protectorem tuum et domnum refugii tui, et putas in caelum conscendisse. Illuderis profecto a phantasia tua, et vana spe consolaris. An putas te usque ad tertium caelum fuisse raptum? Somnia sunt haec! Recordare, obsecro, quam grave peccatum sit ingratitudo. Nonne haec fontem misericordiae exsiccat? Memor esto Dominum flevisse super civitatem Hierusalem, et ei mala ventura praenuntiasse, dicens; 'Quia venient dies in te, et circundabunt te inimici tui vallo, et circundabunt te, coangustabunt te, et ad terram prosternent te et filios tuos qui in te sunt, et non relinquent in te lapidem super lapidem.' Causamque tantorum malorum non tacuit, sed eam subiunxit, dicens: 'Eo quod non cognoveris tempus visitationis tuae.' Ecce quia ingratitudo non modo privari beneficio, sed etiam graviter puniri meretur. Numquid hoc ad animam spectat? Nonne anima in Scripturis per Hierusalem saepius significatur, quae, dum non vult cognoscere visitationem Domini, circundatur a daemonibus et variis temptationibus, quibus angustiata cadit, ad terrena prosternitur, nec in ea virtus aut bonum opus relinquitur

secure. I thank you, good Jesus, for having sent me your Hope, who has lifted me up from the dust and raised me from the dung. She stood me before you so that you might be for me a God who protects and a house of refuge to give me salvation.

My soul is in turmoil! See, Sadness is here. She comes with the banner of justice. She has not retreated from yesterday's battle but is equipped with different weapons, for tonight she made off with my arms and has girded her soldiers with my swords. What shall I do, unarmed and weak? See how aggressively she shouts, with what a great attack she assaults me, how confident she is of victory! "Where is your protector?" she says. "Where is the house of refuge? Where is [your] salvation? Do you still persist in this empty confidence of yours? Those consolations of yours come from your imagination. You have contrived for yourself a God who is gracious and your protector and house of refuge, and you think he has come down from heaven. You really are deluded by your phantasm and consoled by empty Hope. Do you think you have been rapt up to the third heaven? These are dreams! Recall, I ask, what a grave sin is ingratitude. Does it not dry up the fountain of mercy? Remember that the Lord wept over the city of Jerusalem and foretold the evils that would befall her, saying, 'The day will come upon you, and your enemies will surround you with a wall, and encircle you and hem you in, and they will cast down to the ground you and your children who are within you, and they will not leave within you a stone upon a stone' [Luke 19:43-44]. He was not silent about the reason for such great evils, for he added the reason, saying, 'because you did not know the time of your visitation' [Luke 19:44]. See how ingratitude merits not only being deprived of benefits but also undergoing severe punishment. Doesn't this apply to the soul? Doesn't Jerusalem rather often in the Scriptures signify the soul, which when she does not want to recognize the Lord's visitation is surrounded by demons and various temptations? After being besieged, she falls, is cast down to the ground, and no virtue or

quod non destruatur? Omni, enim, gratia privatur, nec de cetero restauratur, quia non cognovit tempus visitationis suae. Tu profecto; tu, inquam, es haec civitas, pluribus et magnis beneficiis a Deo decorata, et non cognovisti ea, sed ingratus fuisti. Ipse te ad imaginem suam creavit; in medio Ecclesiae non inter infideles te genuit; in florida civitate te posuit; aqua baptismi te sanctificavit; in domo religiosa te enutrivit. Tu autem post cogitationes tuas cucurristi; 'in vanitate sensus tui ambulasti,' et in profundum peccatorum devenisti. Dominus te vocabat et non respondebas ei. Saepe te monuit et consilium eius neglexisti. Quotiens te illuminavit; quotiens te ad cor convertit; quotiens de somno excitavit! Invitabat te et tu excusabas; trahebat et tu resistebas ei. Tandem vicit pietas ineffabilis et immensa! Tu peccasti et ipse te visitavit; tu cecidisti et ipse te erexit; tu ignorasti et ipse te docuit; tu caecus fuisti et ipse te illuminavit. A strepitu mundi, a tempestate pelagi te ad quietem et portum religionis perduxit; habitum sanctae conversationis dedit; sacerdotem suum te esse voluit; ad gymnasia suae sapientiae te adduxit. Ingratus tamen semper fuisti et negligenter opus Dei fecisti, cum tamen scires scriptum esse: 'Maledictus qui fecerit opus Dei negligenter.' Nec sic te pietas divina reliquit, sed semper ad meliora benigne provexit et—quod maximum est—te scientia Scripturarum ornavit; sermonem praedicationis in ore tuo posuit et, quasi unum de magnis viris, in medio populi te constituit. Tu, autem, alios docuisti et te ipsum neglexisti; alios curasti et te ipsum non salvasti; 'elevasti cor tuum in decore tuo, ideo perdidisti sapientiam tuam in decore tuo.' Nihili factus es, et nihil eris in perpetuum. An ignoras quia 'servus, sciens voluntatem Domini et non faciens,

good work in her is left without being destroyed. She is deprived of all grace and is not restored in some other way because she did not know the time of her visitation. You precisely. You, I say, are that city, resplendent with many great benefits from God, but you did not acknowledge them but were ungrateful. He created you to his own image. He begot you in the midst of his Church, not among unbelievers. He established you in a prosperous city. He sanctified you with the water of baptism. He nourished you in a religious house. But you chased after your own ideas, 'you walked in the vanity of your way of thinking' [Eph 4:17], and you ended up deep in sins. The Lord kept calling you, but you did not answer him. He warned you often, and you paid no attention to his advice. How often he sent you light, how often he turned you toward your heart, how often he roused you from your sleep! He invited you, and you made excuses. He pulled on you, and you resisted him. Finally his ineffable and limitless kindness won out! You sinned, and he himself visited you. You fell, and he himself raised you up. You were ignorant, and he himself taught you. You were blind, and he himself gave you light. He guided you from the clatter of the world and the storm of the sea to the quiet port of the religious life; he gave you the habit of a holy community life; he wished you to be his priest; he enrolled you in the school of his wisdom. But you were always ungrateful and performed God's work carelessly, even though you knew what is written: 'cursed is the person who did God's work carelessly' [Jer 48:10]. The divine kindness did not leave you at that, but always gently urged you forward to better things and (this is crucial) bestowed on you the knowledge of the Scriptures. It put in your mouth the word of preaching and set you up in the middle of the people as one of the great men. You taught others and neglected yourself. You cured others but did not save yourself. 'Your heart was lifted up in your beauty, so you have lost your wisdom in your beauty' [Ezek 28:17]. You have become nothing, and you will be nothing forever. Are you unaware that 'the ser-

vapulabit multis?' An nescis quia Deus superbis resistit? 'Quomodo cecidisti, Lucifer, qui mane oriebaris, qui vulnerabas gentes, qui dicebas in corde tuo: "in caetum conscendam"?' Verumtamen in infernum detraheris in profundum laci. 'Subter te sternetur tinea, et operimentum tuum erunt vermes.' An putas nunc invenire misericordiam, qui scandalizasti plurimos, qui, totiens a Deo vocatus et monitus, respondere noluisti? Ubi esset iustitia Dei? ubi aequitas iudicii? Non semper prosequitur misericordia peccatorem: terminos sibi statuit. Nonne scriptum est: 'Vocavi et renuistis; expandi manus meas et non fuit qui aspiceret; despexistis omne consilium meum, et increpationes meas neglexistis: ego quoque in interitu vestro ridebo et subsannabo cum vobis id quod timebatis advenerit?' Ecce quia non semper misericordia peccatori dat veniam. An non consideras gradus misericordiae in te finem habere, qui tot beneficiis a Deo honoratus in profundum pelagi cecidisti, qui tot gratiis ornatus ob tuam superbiam et inanem gloriam scandalum fuisti orbis terrarum? Non te itaque decipiat spes vana, quam sequeris. Vive amodo ut libet! Noli in hac et in alia vita poenis infernalibus cruciari! Elige habitare cum his qui ducunt in bonis dies suos et in puncto ad inferna descendunt. Nec pudor te detineat: fac frontem meretricis! 'Comedamus et bibamus: cras enim moriemur!' Desperata est plaga tua: insanabilis facta est!"

Haec cum dixisset, totus exercitus vocibus tremendis ululabat et verba eius etiam repetebat, dicens: "Desperata est plaga tua: insanabilis facta est!" Ego, vero, memor admonitionum matris meae, quamvis aliquantulum animo deiectus, pro viribus erexi me et steti super pedes meos, elevans oculos ad caelum unde

vant who knows his master's will and does not do it will be beaten
with many lashes' [Luke 12:47]? Don't you know that God re-
sists the proud? 'How did you fall, Lucifer, who rose with the
dawn, inflicted wounds on the nations, who said in your heart,
"I will go up into heaven"' [Isa 14:12-13]? 'Instead you will be
dragged down into the depths of the lake in hell' [Isa 14:15].
'The moth will be placed underneath you and worms will be
your covering' [Isa 14:11]. Do you now think that you will find
mercy, you who scandalized many people, you who were unwill-
ing to answer all the times that God called you and warned you?
Where would God's justice be? Where his fairness in judging?
Mercy does not always pursue the sinner; it has set limits for
itself. Is it not written: 'I called, and you refused; I stretched out
my hands, and there was nobody who paid attention'? You have
scorned all my advice and ignored my reproofs. I too will laugh
at your destruction and will mock when what you feared over-
takes you' [Prov 1:24-26]. Note that mercy does not always give
pardon to a sinner. Don't you take account that the degrees of
mercy toward you have a limit, you who were honored by God
with so many benefits, who have fallen into the depths of the sea,
who after being supplied with so many graces have been a scandal to the whole world because of your pride and empty glory? So
don't let empty Hope deceive you so that you follow her. Live
from now on as you please. Resist being tortured in this life and
the other life by hellish punishments! Choose to dwell with those
who spin out their days in good things and in an instant go down
into hell. Don't let shame restrain you: put on the face of a prostitute! 'Let us eat and drink for tomorrow we die' [Isa 22:13].[1]
Your wound is beyond hope; it has become incurable!"

When she had said this, the whole army bellowed out terri-
fying cries and also repeated her words, saying, "Your wound is
beyond hope; it has become incurable!" Mindful of my mother's
warnings, although I was somewhat discouraged in spirit, I drew
myself up as well as I could and stood on my feet and raised my

auxilium expectabam. Et ecce spes, hilari vultu, splendoribus divinis ornata, de alto descendens, ait: "Quae est ista quae 'involvit sententias sermonibus imperitis,' quae posuit terminos misericordiae, quae infinitum vult finire, quae aquas maris in manibus portare se credit? An non audisti Dominum dicentem: In quacumque die ingemuerit peccator, 'omnium iniquitatum eius non recordabor?' Quis est homo qui non peccat? Quis potest dicere: 'mundum est cor meum?' Ad omnes, enim, Oratio Dominica spectat, in qua omnes dicere compelluntur: 'Et dimitte nobis debita nostra.' Apostolos hoc modo Dominus orare docuit. Numquid, ergo, ad caeteros homines haec oratio non pertinebit? Nonne apostoli primitias Spiritus acceperunt? Cur, autem, docuit eos Dominus sic orare, si peccatum non habebant? et, si habebant peccatum, quis poterit gloriari se peccatorem non esse? Audi dilectum discipulum Domini: 'Si dixerimus,' inquit, 'quia peccatum non habemus, nos ipsos seducimus, et veritas in nobis non est.' Et Iacobus apostolus: 'In multis,' ait, 'offendimus omnes.' 'Omnes, ergo, peccaverunt et iugiter egent misericordia Dei' sancti Dei homines. Scriptum est enim: 'Septies in die cadet iustus et resurget.' Non, ergo, misericordia terminos habet; sed quotiescumque peccator ingemuerit, misericordia praesto erit. Nec interest utrum de magnis an de parvis peccatis loquamur. Cecidisti: surge et misericordia te suscipiet. Corruisti: clama et misericordia ad te veniet. Iterum cecidisti, iterum corruisti: convertere ad Dominum et viscera pietatis eius tibi patebunt. Cecidisti, corruisti tertio et quarto: plange et misericordia non te derelinquet. Quotiens peccas, totiens resurge, et misericordia finem non habebit. Ut quid improperas beneficia accepta, O feminarum pessima, tristitia? An non David, propheta maximus, magna et multa beneficia accepit, de quo dixit Dominus: 'Inveni virum secundum cor meum'? Et tamen peccavit, et quidem graviter, tam in adulterio quam in homicidio iusti viri et innocentis. Nec

eyes toward heaven, from which I was looking for help. Behold, Hope with smiling face and adorned with divine splendors was coming down from above and saying, "What is this, 'which has wrapped ideas in inept terms' [Job 38:2], which has set limits to mercy, which wants to make finite the infinite, which believes that it can carry the waters of the sea in its hands? Didn't you hear the Lord saying that in whatsoever day the sinner shall sigh, 'I will not remember all his iniquities' [Ezek 18:22]? What person is there who does not sin? Who can say, 'my heart is clean'? The Lord's Prayer applies to all; in it all are obliged to say 'and forgive us our trespasses' [Matt 6:12]. This is how the Lord taught the apostles to pray. Shall this prayer not be applicable to other people? Did not the apostles receive the first fruits of the Spirit? Why then did the Lord teach them to pray that way if they did not have sin? And if they had sin, who will be able to boast that he is not a sinner? Listen to the beloved disciple of the Lord: 'If we were to say,' he says, 'that we do not have sin, we are fooling ourselves, and the truth is not in us' [1 John 1:8]. And the apostle James says, 'We offend in many things' [Jas 3:2]. The holy ones of God 'all have sinned and stand ever in need of God's' [Rom 3:23] mercy. It is written: 'The just person will fall seven times a day and will get up again' [Prov 24:16]. Mercy then has no limits, but as often as the sinner sighs, mercy will be at hand. Nor does it matter if we are talking about great or small sins. You have fallen; get up and mercy will welcome you. You toppled: call and mercy will come to you. You fell again, you toppled again: turn to the Lord and the heart of his kindness will be opened for you. You fell, you toppled a third and fourth time; wail out and mercy will not desert you. As often as you sin, so often arise, and mercy will not have a limit. O Sadness, worst of women, why are you throwing out taunts about benefits received? Did not David, the greatest of prophets, receive many great benefits? The Lord spoke of him: 'I have found a man after my own heart' [Acts 13:22]. Yet he sinned, and sinned seriously, both by adultery and by murder-

tamen Dominus suam misericordiam in eo terminavit. Quid
superbiae peccatum adducis? Nonne ipse David elevavit cor suum,
et numerare fecit populum Israel? Gloriabatur, enim, quasi rex
magnus et potens, in virtute sua; nec tamen ob hoc reprobatus
est. Quare? Quia peccatum suum non abscondit. Non illud
praedicavit sicut Sodoma, sed dixit: 'Confitebor adversum me
iniustitiam meam Domino.' Misericordia, itaque, non sibi
terminos posuit, sed reprobi statuunt sibi fines ut ad eos non
transeat: nam usque ad terminos eorum vadit, sed ipsi repellunt
eam. Hinc scriptum est: 'Perditio tua, Israel: ex me tantummodo
auxilium tuum.' 'Aperi os tuum,' inquit misericordia, 'et implebo
illud; expande sinum tuum et dabo tibi "mensuram bonam et
coagitatam et supereffluentem".' Persiste in orationibus et fletu,
quia qui coepit te diligere et beneficiis gratiisque te ad suum
amorem provocare, non deficiet sed magis perciet opus suum.
Quaenam causa naturalis incipit opus ut in medio itineris desistat?
Virtus seminis non cessat donec fructus ad perfectionem perveniat.
Quae avis relinquit pullos suos antequam se ipsos regere valeant?
Cur hoc faciunt? Quae utilitas ex hoc provenit illis? Nulla profecto,
sed tantum labor. Amor, ergo, cogit naturales causas suos effectus
ad perfectum perducere. Bonitas compellit eas, quam cupiunt
diffundere: bonum enim est sui ipsius diffusivum. Si hoc faciunt
creaturae, quid faciet Creator? Ipse enim amor est; ipse bonitas
infinita. An non perficiet opus suum? Audi Dominum Iesum:
'Mea,' inquit, 'voluntas "est ut faciam voluntatem eius qui misit
me ut perficiam opus eius".' Qui, ergo, coepit te amare, te suis
beneficiis et gratiis attrahere, te a peccatis mundare, procul dubio
perficiet opus suum. Haec enim sunt praeparationes aeternae vitae. Cur, igitur, nunc cadens, non es collisus? Nonne quia
Dominus supposuit manum suam? Quare convertit ad se cor
tuum? Cur te ad paenitentiam provocavit? Cur consolatus est te?

ing a just and innocent man. But God did not cut off his mercy toward him. Why do you bring up the sin of pride? Did not David become puffed up in heart and have the people of Israel counted? Like a great and mighty king, he boasted of his power, but he still was not reprobated for that. Why? Because he did not hide his sin. He did not proclaim it like Sodom, but he said, 'I confess against myself my injustice to the Lord' [Ps 32:5]. Mercy then does not set limits for itself but the reprobate establish their own boundaries so that mercy cannot come over to them, for it comes right up to their limits, but they drive it back. Hence it is written: 'Your death is your own, Israel; from me comes only help for you' [Hos 13:9]. Mercy says, 'Open your mouth and I will fill it, make room in your bosom, and I will give you "good measure, shaken together and flowing over" [Luke 6:38].' Persevere in prayer and weeping because the person who begins to love you and challenge you to his love with benefits and graces does not cut short but even more stirs up his work. What natural cause starts a work so as to stop in mid course? The power of a seed does not stop until its fruit reaches to perfection. What bird leaves her chicks before they can take care of themselves? Why do they do this? What advantage do they get from this? None at all, but only labor. Love then drives natural causes to carry through their effects to completion. Goodness, which they desire to spread aboard, forces them: goodness tends to spread itself out. If creatures do this, what will the Creator do? He himself is love. He himself is infinite goodness. Will he not complete his work? Listen to the Lord Jesus. He says, 'My will "is that I do the will of him who sent me so that I may complete his work" [John 4:34].' So he who began to love you, to attract you with his gifts and graces, to wash you from your sins, will undoubtedly complete his work. These are preparations for eternal life. Now when you fall, why are you not smashed? Isn't it because the Lord has put his hand under you? Why has he converted your heart to himself? Why has he provoked you to repentance? Why did he con-

Nonne ut te mundet, et gratia sua dignum faciat, et ad vitam aeternam perducat? Non sunt haec illusiones aut imaginationes tuae, sed divinae inspirationes. Sed esto imaginationes sint. Nonne bonae sunt? Nonne de fidei virtute proveniunt? Cum itaque omne bonum a Deo sit, utique sunt hae imaginationes divinae illuminationes. Exulta, ergo, in verbis istis!"

Ad haec verba adeo confortatum est cor meum quod prae gaudio psallere coepi, dicens: "Dominus illuminatio mea et salus mea, quem timebo? Dominus protector vitae meae, a quo trepidabo?", et ad pedes Domini cum lacrimis provolutus, dixi: "Domine, si consistant adversum me castra, non timebit cor meum!"

"Quoniam fortitudo mea et refugium meum es tu, et propter nomen tuum deduces me, et enutries me." ....

sole you? Was it not so that he might wash you, make you worthy
of his grace, and lead you to life everlasting? These are not your
delusions and fantasies but divine inspirations. Suppose they are
fantasies. Are they not good? Do they not stem from the virtue of
faith? Since every good comes from God, these fantasies are indeed divine illuminations. Rejoice then in these words!"

My heart was so comforted by these words that I began to
sing for joy, saying: "The Lord is my light and my salvation, whom
shall I fear? The Lord is the protector of my life, of whom shall I
be afraid" [Ps 27:1]? In tears I threw myself down at the Lord's
feet and said, "Lord, should an armed camp stand against me,
my heart will not fear" [Ps 27:3]!

"For you are my strength and my refuge, and for your name's
sake you will lead me and nourish me" [Ps 31:3]. ....

NOTES

1. This passage and the previous temptations to disbelief and suicide urged by Sadness gave rise to a disagreement between the
French scholar Robert Klein and the Soviet M. Goukowski.
In his "La dernière méditation de Savonarola," *Bibliothèque
d'Humanisme et Renaissance* 23 (1961) 441-48, Klein pointed
out how similar temptations were seen as attacking the dying
in the abundant *Ars moriendi* literature of the fifteenth century, which may have served Savonarola as a source. Goukowski
in his "Réponse à M. Robert Klein" *Ibid.* 25 (1963), 222-26
[to which Klein responded, *Ibid.* 226-27], noted that
Savonarola's sources may rather be real currents of unbelief
and Epicureanism which were not rare among Italian intellec-
tuals of his time. Goukowski saw these doubts and temptations as much more than mere literary straw men for Savonarola. On this point I side with Klein, for it is Hope which has

the last word in Savonarola's meditation, even if her arguments
may not carry conviction for many twentieth-century readers.
Moreover, Savonarola's exposition of this Psalm was cut short
by his execution. Psalm 30 (31), on which he chose to reflect,
goes on to describe how the psalmist is scorned by his enemies, dreaded by his acquaintances, and surrounded by plots
against his life until he becomes "like a broken vessel" [Ps 31:
11-13]. But the Psalm ends by proclaiming trust in God, who
protects those who fear him from the plots of men, preserves
the faithful and requites the proud [19-23]. Savonarola's
broader relation to the *Ars moriendi* tradition has also been
explored by Donald Weinstein, "*The Art of Dying Well* and
Popular Piety in the Preaching and Thought of Girolamo
Savonarola," in *Life and Death in Fifteenth-Century Florence*,
Marcel Tetel, et al., eds. (Durham, NC: Duke University Press,
1989) 89-104.